Esoteric Science, Volume 2

J.S. Williams

ISBN: 0615837522
ISBN-13: 978-0615837529 (Conscious_Creations)

To the youthful revolution that approaches.

CONTENTS

FOREWORD

Upon the publication of this book, author J.S. Williams will be 21 years old. When I was 21 years old, though my quest for an understanding of this world was well underway, my actual comprehension of the subjects that I would later come to familiarize myself with, adore and embrace were merely seeds in my mind, planted within the soil of my soul that had not yet quite taken root. Only through years of study, self-reflection, failures and triumphs did I finally start to nourish those seeds with the waters of my own personal heaven and the light of truth within the kingdom of my temple. It would take many years of whittling down the rough and jagged edges of my imperfect self, carving out the spiritual David lying beneath the monolith of my ignorance, digging deep within the darkness of my inner landscape, and traversing my own spiritual vistas to even come close to discovering who I was, what my purpose in this life is and what kind of moral code and conduct I intended to live by. At age

21, I was more concerned with chasing skirts, rebelling for the sake of rebelling and upholding my own overblown and indignant ego, than I was trying to search for the god who dwelled within. I certainly did not have myself together enough to pen my first, *let alone second,* book. I certainly did not have the candor, gumption and maturity to recognize the dragon that I had to slay and the spiritual mountain in which I was to climb and I certainly, unlike Mr. Williams, did not have a full enough comprehension of these ideas that I could have written the book that you are holding in your hands right now.

The broadening of our definition of acceptable science is currently underway in our culture and a revolution of mind is taking place. There can be no doubt that the World Wide Web, the interconnectivity of human beings on a global scale, the ushering in of the information age and the perceived quickening and concrescence of events within our time have all played an enormous part in widening the spectrum of our definition of existence. Currently, our models of acceptable science, with reductionism and materiality leading the charge, are profoundly lacking and this almost deranged focus on the corporeal aspects of our reality are leaving many questions unanswered. Though the modern scientific paradigm, without a doubt, has made its own advances, it has also left us bereft when it comes to comprehending the human experience as it is. The modern scientific method has basically nothing to say about human consciousness and the human being's place in the universe, except to say that it is, essentially, *meaningless.* Divinity, inherent purpose and the conscious intelligence within nature have been almost entirely drained from the contemporary perspective, and the neoteric institutions carving out the approved mindset have taken a strong hold on the imaginations of several generations.

Mythology, theology, spirituality, psychology and philosophy have been placed on the back-burner, with the temperature dial turned in the off-position, letting the magic and magnificence of the high wisdom of our elders grow cold. Modernity has gone so far as to call the ancients and their stories, symbols and mythological creatures the fabrications of superstitious and primitive minds, people merely seeking meaning in a meaningless world. "Were our ancestors imaginative? Yes. Scientific? No."

Mr. Williams makes the case that the abandonment of the esoteric has left us bewildered to our true calling and that the focus on the exoteric has left the perennial fruits of human wisdom lain to rot on the wayside of the road of life.

Like Campbell, Jung, Eliade, Kuhn, and so many others before him, J.S. Williams has taken it upon himself to refuel and pass on the torch of truth, using every faculty of the mind, body and soul to come to a full understanding of the ancient mindset and the sophistication of thought that permeated antiquity. As he details, very concisely in this volume, this mindset is alive and well and at work in our modern world. The archetypes, symbols and mystical quests crafted into myth after myth, having strong commonalities worldwide despite vast geographic divisions, underlie the varying garments of thought woven by the myriad civilizations and religions throughout time. These mythologies and tales represent cosmological principles, whether we choose to recognize them or not, that play out in our very lives, right now. These stories and concepts are considered *timeless* because they indeed *transcend all time*. Death and resurrection, sacrifice, slaying the dragon and reincarnation are all themes that find their way into culture after culture because these elements are part of the lattice work of the archetypal world of the imagination and the collective unconscious of man. These are not stories invented and crafted by a particular culture or a certain religion for existential sake but rather stories that concretize the foundation of every life that has graced this blessed Earth. They glorify the human being and elucidate his or her true divine nature. They stir the coals of the imagination and set fire to the spirit. They carve out the path for the hero's journey and ask one to take the first steps forward on this path. They represent the merging of the esoteric with the exoteric, the spirit with the matter and the above with the below. They present the individual with the framework to understand his or her wholeness and place in the grand cosmic schema. They may very well be the universal panacea mankind has so been desperately and aimlessly searching for in the darkness of his own philistinism.

Placing one foot in the ethereal and the other in the material, J.S. Williams takes a firm stance in recognizing that the truth lies somewhere within the balance of both. His pursuit is not anchored in bias or belief, but with clear eyes on alethiology. Realizing that modernity can no longer suffer under the weight of its strict material worldview, he has decided to take this noble stand for the betterment and advancement of our comprehension of the world and has done so beautifully in these volumes.

Expect big things from Mr. Williams. His passion, sincerity, determination, open-mindedness and commitment to a true understanding of our world shine through in his work. J.S. Williams is not only noble and committed enough to recognize his own mystical, heroic epic and the dragons that he must slay, he is well-versed and advanced enough in his understanding of this archetypal, mythological world that he is in the position, even at such a young age, to be able to give you some pointers in how to do this in your own life. I look forward to Volume 3. I could have used a J.S. Williams when I was 21. Hell, I could use a J.S. Williams when I am 91.

Marty Leeds

Author of Pi – The Great Work

Pi & The English Alphabet Vol. 1

Pi & The English Alphabet Vol. 2

Albany, Wisconsin

INTRODUCTION

This essay will be split into three parts: "Mythos," "Pathos," and "Logos." As one may note, ethos is omitted—the egocentric idea of the appeal to authority is anachronistic—a work should speak for itself with no introductory badges needed. Thus, to follow the theme of the essay, the far more intriguing mode of persuasion shall once again be known—that is *mythos*. The first part of this essay looks into patterns in comparative mythology with a focus on the heroic tales. The central motif is the identification of what has been termed archetypes. For those readers who have not been initiated into the academics' idea for the modes of persuasion, pathos is the appeal to the audience's emotions, which is often done via metaphors and analogies; logos is the logical appeal to the audience—facts and figures. Accordingly, Part Two, "Pathos," will demonstrate how the archetypes have manifested in the works of the two most well-known heroic myth tellers of today, J.R.R. Tolkien and J.K. Rowling. Analogies and metaphors will be used to exemplify this. The last part, "Logos," will bring all of these myths into a logical understanding by showing historical people who have become, or embodied, the heroic archetype. This will be done by looking into figures of the counterculture movement of the 1960s and 70s.

In *Volume 1* we learned the importance of the symbol in esotericism—that it has a magical substratum to it. No less shall the symbol be used in this current volume. For that reason, we must make sure the symbol is fully understood for the context that it will be used throughout this essay. A symbol can mean anything. As Robert Anton Wilson would have said, "Which reality tunnel are you viewing the symbol from?" For one person it could mean this and for another that. However, in this book we will see that there is a probabilistic scale for what the symbol is truly trying to represent. That is, a certain symbol will have a high probability of transferring the same meaning to multiple people. In effect, one can contemplate the symbol and the clues that arise from it to discern the highest probability for what the symbol is truly representing. However, this is relevant only to the reality tunnel in which the symbol is being viewed from. If the reality tunnel is clogged by the status quo, then it may need to be drained so that the tunnel is not so narrowly open to its reality. I need not remind the reader of all of the ideas that the status quo has suppressed throughout history, which later became held as empirical ideas.

PART ONE
Mythos

1 ARCHETYPES

"It is the inevitable fate of physics, which operates with statistical laws of nature, that it has to strive for completeness. But in so doing, it will necessarily come up against the psychology of the unconscious, since precisely what it lacks is this unconscious and the psyche of the observer. Just as physics seeks completeness, your analytical psychology seeks a home. For there is no denying the fact that psychology, like an illegitimate child of the spirit, leads an esoteric, special existence beyond the fringe of what is generally acknowledged to be the academic world. But this is how the archetype of the coniunctio is constellated. Whether and when this coniunctio will be realized I do not know, but I am in no doubt at all that this would be the finest fate that could happen to both physics and psychology."
— Nobel laureate Wolfgang Pauli to Carl Jung[1]

---

[1] *Atom and Archetype: The Pauli/Jung Letters, 1932-1958* by Wolfgang Pauli and Carl Jung, pg. 122 (Princeton University Press, 2001)

There are two definitions for the word *archetype* that resound in the topic of esotericism. These definitions were coined by two of the most important scholars of 20th century academia: the renowned psychologist, Carl Jung, and arguably the most significant religious studies professor of the last century, Mircea Eliade.

For the former, "The primordial image, or archetype, is a figure—be it a daemon, a human being, or a process—that constantly recurs in the course of history and appears wherever creative fantasy is freely expressed."[2] In this way, Jung saw archetypes as inherent codes embedded into the collective unconscious.[3] In other words, in the psyche of every human being exist archetypal energies that direct, or influence, this individual; albeit the personal conscious of this individual—for the most part—is never aware of these archetypes in their entirety. With this definition, an archetype is a phenomenon of psychology— something that *occurs within the microcosm.*

For the latter, Eliade uses the archetype in a more cosmological sense rather than psychologically—he uses it "[...] just as Eugenio d'Ors does, as a synonym for 'exemplary model' or 'paradigm.'"[4] In his view, archetypes are symbols, or even life-forces, from the metaphysical realm(s) which produced this physical world. His premise is venerated due to the fact that in ancient civilizations and shamanic tribal societies, the same archetypal patterns occur—despite geographical isolation—as we

---

[2] *The Portable Jung* by Carl Jung, pg. 319 (The Viking Press, 1974)
[3] Ibid, pg. 60
[4] *Cosmos and History* by Mircea Eliade, pg. ix (Harper Touchbooks, 1959)

touched upon in *Esoteric Science, Volume 1*. For example, Eliade shows that it cannot be coincidence that the ancient cities in Babylon, Egypt, Israel, India, Tibet, and so on, were built to align with the cosmos. He implies that the cosmological archetypes influenced the individuals' psyches in each different region, directing them in the construction of these star maps, making this pattern occur. As his definition for an archetype is cosmological, it is a phenomenon that *occurs within the macrocosm*.

One may say that these definitions go off on two different tangents, but what if they are really intertwined? What if they are both different "aspects" attempting to describe one and the same thing?

The quantum mechanical approach to understand what this exactly means would be esotericism. This is because of what is termed "entanglement" in quantum mechanics. "The world of quantum mechanics—the base upon which the world we see it built—is composed of entities that are either, in the jargon of physics, not *locally causal*, not *fully separable*, or even not *real unless observed*."[5] Meaning, everything is attached together in some sort of mysterious matrix that is somehow activated by the observer through consciousness. Correspondingly, a fundamental principle in esotericism is the understanding that everything is within and without the microcosm. Thus, just as there are archetypes within each individual, there are archetypes without each individual—in nature, the cosmos, the higher realms, etc. They are all connected together—entanglement.

Both Jung and Eliade were highly concerned that humanity

---

[5] *The Age of Entanglement* by Louisa Gilder, pg. 9 (Vintage Books, 2009)

is no longer living in the myth. However, when studying both Jung and Eliade, one sees that they completely lived in the myth. Both individuals had open-enough-minds to look outside the dogma of the Western world-view to try to understand reality in a more unified manner. Jung looked into alchemy and hermetic philosophy, ancient religions, eastern mysticism, and even theosophy for attempting to understand psychology. He visited both America and Africa to live with the tribal people, and he studied the way of the shaman, or medicine-man, living in these tribes. In effect, he discerned that the philosophical views of the shamans were very in par with his own, but based on less intellectual rhetoric and more on symbolic terminology. In a sense, Jung even was a shaman himself. Cambridge scholar, Joseph Campbell, reports what Jung's *being* caused very early on in his career:

"A middle-aged woman on crutches came into the room one day, led by a maid. She had for seventeen years been suffering a painful paralysis of the left leg; and when he had placed her in a comfortable chair, bidding her tell her story, she went on at such interminable length that he had to finally interrupt. 'Well now,' [Jung] said, 'we have no more time for talk[;] I am now going to hypnotize you.' Whereupon she closed her eyes and fell into a profound trance without any hypnosis at all, continuing, meanwhile, her talking, relating the most remarkable dreams. The situation for the baffled young instructor, before his twenty students, was becoming increasingly uncomfortable; and when he tried to wake her, without success, he became alarmed. It took some ten minutes to bring her to, and when she woke, she was giddy and confused. He said to her, 'I am the doctor; everything is all right.' At which she cried out, 'But I am cured!' threw away her crutches, and was able to walk."[6]

All one needs to do is pick up any of Eliade's books to understand that he knew there to be underlying patterns in one specific culture with all the rest. These men were two peas in a pod. In fact, in *Shamanism*, Eliade identifies that the shamans who've shown up on every continent, send their patients into a trance state in order to cure serious injuries, illnesses, and diseases—just as Jung did as a young man (pun intended).

As these "two peas in a pod" were able to look at the world—in the same perspective as Isaac Newton did[7]—as a philosophical treasure hunt, their understanding of archetypal forces in the universe could not have been more spot on for their time.

In the afterword of *Volume 1* of this study, that is, the transition into this current volume, we saw that Viracocha, Quetzalcoatl, Siddhartha Gauatama, Jesus Christ, Lao Tzu, and Balinas all have very similar stories. Each story demonstrates a "savior." But that is not the proper term; each of these individuals were revolutionaries—they changed the times that they lived in into something better than before (at least in the local geographical area). Each individual also demonstrated supernatural abilities, in many cases the ability to heal at will—in a similar fashion as Jung, although as the myths have it, a lot more efficiently than Jung. They also brought vast knowledge to people, aiming to expand others' consciousness. Lastly, the phenomenon of the spirit or soul ascending to heaven after death comes up in each case. Here ascension is rather a symbol, meaning after

---

[6] *The Portable Jung* by Carl Jung, pg. xiv (The Viking Press, 1974)
[7] See: *Esoteric Science, Volume 1* by J.S. Williams, pgs. 156-8 (Conscious_Creations, 2012)

becoming the "hero" they evolved, or ascended to a higher level of existence symbolized by the spirit flying upwards to the heavens.

As each case demonstrates congruities, this implies that these individuals embodied a certain archetype or archetypes that are embedded into the psychology of humankind—within the microcosm—and after doing so they became an archetype that is within the macrocosm symbolized by the ascension. At this point, so-called "Christians" would argue that Jesus was no man—they'd proclaim, "He's the Son of God!!" Well, Jesus said, "For I have given you an example, that ye should do as I have done" (John 13 : 15). Perhaps it is time to become the son (or daughter) of God, as well? Again, a man once asked Balinas "[...] in what manner the gods were to be worshipped? He answered, as masters (i.e. what one should strive to become). Then how heroes? and he said as fathers (i.e. how one should model themselves in order to become a master)" (parenthesis are mine).[8] In a more precise explanation, Siddhartha said, "Be, now, each one of you, your own torch; look to no one to bring you light. He (or she) who is his (or her) own torch, after I have left the world, will show that he (or she) has understood the meaning of my words; he (or she) will be my true disciple" (parenthesis are mine).[9] After synthesizing these three quotes into a general understanding, one sees that they are advising us to embody an archetype, or multiple archetypes, within ourselves, as they clearly appear to have done within themselves.

---

[8] *The Life of Apollonius of Tyana* by Philostrophus, edited by Edward Berwick, pg. 225
[9] *The Life of Buddha* by Andre-Ferdinand Herold, pg. 227 (Forgotten Books, 1929)

As was shown in the last volume, we saw that we are currently in the transition out of the Pisces (fish) constellation predominantly influencing life on Earth in relation to the precession of the equinoxes. Thus, Christianity, the symbol of the fish, has been the hegemonic figure. However, what Christianity was at its beginning is far different from what it has become. Christ emerged out of Israel, the amalgamation of Semitics, Arabians, and Africans alike. Thus, it is very interesting to look into the Judeo-Christian documents that we have recently unearthed—some of the oldest of the Judeo-Christian documents.

Harvard University provides images with a translation of the most recent finding, discovered in 2012.[10] This finding has been entitled "The Gospel of Jesus' Wife," and it was written in Coptic, the written and spoken language of Egypt during the time of Christ. In this Gospel, Jesus explains that he has a wife and that she is just as able to be his disciple as anybody else.

The next finding has its location in twelve caves in Israel. *The Dead Sea Scrolls* were discovered between 1946-1956, and what they reveal is an echo of the events that took place. One of the first scholars to examine *The Dead Sea Scrolls*, Oxford Professor Geza Vermes, writes, "The large majority of experts holds that the three elements [of the Scrolls] are interconnected and that at least some of the literary works are of Essene origin."[11] Who really were the original Christians?

need to read

---

[10] See: "The Gospel of Jesus's Wife: A New Coptic Gospel Papyrus" at http://www.hds.harvard.edu/faculty-research/research-projects/the-gospel-of-jesuss-wife
[11] *Out of the Cave: A Philosophical Inquiry into the Dead Sea Scrolls Research* by Geza Vermes, in the academic Journal Common Knowledge, Volume 16 (Spring 2010)

When looking into the original Christians, we arrive at the Essenes, the Therapeutae, and the Gnostics. All three groups were highly ascetic, using solitude as a vehicle for spiritual experiences. These groups did not conflict with each other. Instead, they were rather very similar movements but in slightly different geographical areas; although, in some cases, they were in the same place.

To stay with the *rhythmos*, the flow, the Essenes will be illustrated first. The Essenes spoke Hebrew, they lived in voluntary poverty, they practiced abstinence from worldly affairs, they forbade the expression of anger, they were devoted to charity, they were well-learnt on all the various angels (i.e. spiritual beings), they were secret keepers, they used water for a daily purification ritual, and in many cases practiced celibacy. This just so happens to be fundamentally the same thing as Buddhism and other Eastern traditions. (Note that the angels are in correspondence with Eastern deities in this case). Due to this, in the past, this group of writers has argued that Christianity "birthed" Buddhism, and that group of writers has argued that Buddhism "birthed" Christianity. We will just stay in tune with the great mind of Mircea Eliade, and recognize that this is a common destination for a person or peoples with spiritual motives and neither birthed the other *per se*. For if you look into the shamanic tribes found on every continent, these same modalities generally sum up the lifestyle of the ascetic shaman in each of these cultures.

We are left with some characteristics of the Essenes. Josephus the Jew, who lived from 37-100 A.D., is regarded as one of the most important ancient sources on the Essenes.[12] Classist Professor G.A. Williamson writes, "[Josephus'] aim was to rehabilitate his people in the eyes of their Roman conquerors, who [...] were genuinely interested in their curious beliefs and customs, but through grievous misunderstanding were prone to despise them."[13] The Essenes held this view. As we will see, their conflict with Rome is shared with the other original Christians.

The Therapeutae were the Christians inhabiting the lands of Egypt directly after the time of Christ. The Hellenistic Jew Philo Judaeus lived from 20 B.C. to 50 A.D. in Egypt. From Philos' writings we learn that the Therapeutae are called "the Philosophers." He "Applauds the Essenes and Therapeutae for their refusal to have slaves. [...] but he was clearly not ready to commit [to their way of life]."[14] He explains that the Therapeutae devoted much time to contemplation and self-discipline, and although he idolized this lifestyle he was not completely ready for it.[15] The Therapeutae lived a *lavrite* lifestyle,[16] which is defined as "A cluster of cells or caves laid out for hermit monks, having in common a centre containing a church and sometimes a

[12] *Josephus' Description of the Essenes Illustrated by the Dead Sea Scrolls* by Todd Beall, pg. 2 (Cambridge University Press, 2004)

[13] *The world of Josephus* by Geoffrey Arthur Williamson, pg. 283 (Secker &Warburg, 1964)

[14] *A Brief Guide to Philo* by Kenneth Schenck, pg. 68 (Westminster John Knox Press, 2005)

[15] Ibid, pg. 66

[16] *Cyclopaedia of biblical, theological and ecclesiastical literature, Volume 10* by John McClintock and James Strong, pg. 339 (Harper & Bros., 1891)

refectory."[17]

Instantly, we are reminded of the four schools of Tibet—the three branches of the Red Hats, and the branch of the Yellow Hats; or the six schools of philosophies of Vedic India; or the four centers in ancient Egypt: Heliopolis, Thebes, Memphis, and Hermopolis. In each location these groups were in harmony with each other—they were different aspects of the same way of life, but were separated by grades in spiritual advancement/understanding. In these areas, the hermit-life was the ideal psychological existence, and each also had the Jesus-like revolutionary hero as its empowering symbol: Tonpa Shenrab Miwoche in Tibet (the Central Asian Buddha, far older than Siddhartha), Siddhartha Gautama/Krishna in India, and Osiris/Horus in Egypt. Due to the nature of the Therapeutae, we don't really know too much more about them—they were secret holders as well.

We do know a good amount about the Gnostics, as they were the ones publishing new Gospels on a regular basis. In a peer-reviewed article by Professor Edward Moore, it is shown that Gnosticism is a child, or product, of Hermeticism.[18] In *Volume 1*, it was shown that Sigmund Freud saw all Abrahamic religions to be byproducts of Hermeticism, but the Gnostics' cosmology perhaps demonstrates this the most vividly. The word Gnostic comes from two Greek words: *gnōsis,* or "knowledge," and *gnostikos,* meaning "the learned." The Gnostics saw Jesus Christ to be the primal man, or model. Eipiphaniues wrote about the Gnostic Ebionites, saying

---

[17] *Early Christian and Byzantine Architecture* by Richard Krautheimer, pg. 519 (Yale University Press, 1992)
[18] See: *Gnosticism* by Edward Moore at http://www.iep.utm.edu/gnostic/

that they "[...] invoked 'heaven and earth, salt and water, winds and 'angels of righteousness' in cases of illness. The point of this reference is that the elements here invoked along with the angels are not too far removed from the Epedoclean, (the elemental spirits of the universe)" (parenthesis are mine).[19] In other words, there was intercommunication between what Eliade defines as the cosmological archetypes and the Gnostics, and they used the symbol of Jesus Christ as their model for attaining spiritual enlightenment. Despite worshipping elemental spirits they recognized the archetypes as coming from a monad, or singular source—just as did the Egyptians, Tibetans, and Indians.

When looking deeper into the Gnostics, we find that they had a very quantum mechanical outlook on reality. They were filled with an urge, or passion, to dedicate much of their time in trying to understand how the world and universe has manifested. They believed that coming out of the singular source were divine beings called *Aeons*, which were different aspects of the one source that appear in dualistic qualities—feminine and masculine, positive and negative, light and dark, and so on. These *Aeons* then produced further dualistic principles, *Demiurge*, the *Ogdoad*, *Archons,* and so forth.[20] The *Demiurge* is a masculine deity, who was held as the creator of this physical world. The *Demiurge's* creation, however, is really an illusion—they viewed the physical world as a hologram of a metaphysical existence—in the same way that Plato saw physical reality to only be "shadows projected on a cave's wall," and Newton and Leibniz viewed the physical world as "mechanistic" in illusion and metaphysical in nature.

---

[19] *Colossians and Philemon* by Robert Wilson, pg. 39 (Continuum, 2005)
[20] *Gnosticism: Beliefs and Practices* by John Harris, pg. 108 (Sussex Academic Press, 1999)

Ogdoad often refers to the Mother principle coming from the one source, but sometimes it is used as a multi-deification of a common principle that is not necessarily only feminine.[21] The Archons are high spiritual beings, those of the stars and the planets in our solar system.

The important aspect of the Gnostics' cosmology is that the feminine is in unison with the masculine. Violet MacDermot writes in *The Fall of Sophia,*

> "There are three principal characterizations of the divine feminine in early Gnostic writings. The first of these perceives the highest Godhead as a dyad of masculine and feminine elements, wherein the feminine component is represented as an eternal, mystic Silence. The second sees the Holy Spirit as feminine, thus including the female element in the Holy Trinity, which in most Gnostic myths represents the Godhead in manifestation. The third is the characterization of the Holy Sophia, as found in *Pistis Sophia* and cognate Gnostic works."[22]

This embodiment of the feminine reveals the true nature of the original Christians—just as the Coptic document unearthed in 2012 reveals the true nature of Christ's views on the feminine.

Due to the Gnostics' more reasonable approach to cosmology—that is, the understanding that there is both the feminine and the masculine—what we are left with from the Gnostics is several writings describing personal spiritual experiences—such as leaving the physical body via the

---

[21] Ibid, pg. 172
[22] *The Fall of Sophia* by Violet MacDermot (SteinerBooks, 2002)

soul/spirit—in a very poetic manner.[23] The reason that I say that these experiences are due to this cosmological outlook is that many of the other cultures with records describing the same out-of-body-experiences also embraced the feminine.[24] Thus, the Gnostics appear to truly be "the learned"—the ones who received *gnosis* from metaphysical reality. As it is obvious that there is feminine everywhere we look, this indicates that there are feminine archetypes in metaphysical reality. As such, they came to realize the contrasts between dualisms, and in particular the contrast between good and evil. They were philosophers, just as the Therapeutae and the Essenes were.

> "Evil resides in the body, which is but a semblance as opposed to reality, in the impermanent as opposed to the eternal, thus breaching an infinite gulf between evil and good. Gnosis has a redemptive function of delivering [human] from this stranglehold of evil until his (or her) soul is completely illumined with the celestial light of truth." (parenthesis are mine)[25]

Sounds a lot like the story of Jesus Christ—does it not?

Now what we are left with to ponder is: what the hell happened to the original Christians? How did what was practically the same thing as 'Buddhahood' become a patriarchal, organized religion that is known for massive amounts of oppression throughout its timeline? The answer is rather ironic.

---

[23] *Gnosis* by Dan Merkur, pg. 64 (State University of New York Press, 1993)
[24] See: *Esoteric Science, Volume 1* by J.S. Williams (Conscious_Creations, 2012)
[25] Ibid.

If the effect was Jesus Christ and his teachings becoming popular, then the cause was the Roman hegemony oppressing the geographical area. In 200 B.C., the Roman Empire controlled what is modern-day Italy and the eastern part of Spain. In the 200 years following, the Western Roman Empire conquered nearly the entire Mediterranean—Southern Europe, Northern Africa, and Western Asia Minor. During this expansion, the Romans enslaved the people that they conquered. Enslavement was definitely not started by the Romans, but their slavery had a very pompous cruelty to it. For instance, L. Pedanius Scundus, a Roman elite, supposedly got killed by one of his slaves and the Roman courts then executed all of the other 400 slaves in the household.[26] Rome was also highly patriarchal—not even elite women were allowed to vote or hold a public office.[27] "The success of Rome flowed from obedience to authority, especially paternal and state authority."[28] Take a mental note—paternal and state authority will unveil its mask again shortly.

In *Relations Between the Ego and the Unconscious*, Jung shows that when one has gone through much suffering and then has a realization able to transcend this suffering, inflation or expansion of consciousness generally follows. Jung writes, "He is hypnotized [by this realization], and instantly believes he has solved the riddle of the universe."[29] In authoritarian Rome, King Herod the so-called "Great" was the puppet of Rome watching

---

[26] *Clemency and Cruelty in the Roman World* by Melissa Dowling, pg. 211 (University of Michigan Press, 2006)
[27] *The Cambridge Companion to the Age of Augustus* edited by Karl Galinsky, pg. 198 (Cambridge University Press, 2005)
[28] *Patriarchy, Property and Death in the Roman Family* by Richard Saller, pg. 106 (Cambridge University Press, 1996)
[29] *The Portable Jung*, by Carl Jung, pg. 104 (The Viking Press, 1974)

over Judea during the time of Christ. Herod was a polygamist and a brute—he liked to send the heads off of his protesting adversaries.[30] Then Christ came along—most likely thinking all of this was imprudent at the very least—and started suggesting that the people should love thy neighbor, repent wrongdoings, encourage the oppressed, feed the poor, and seek justice. Suddenly, the people started having realizations. The realizations then brought about an inflation of consciousness. The poor and the rich, alike, realized that ending their suffering had to do with how they treated each other. Rome, who saw its clench of control diminishing by the very act of love, then nailed Jesus to the Cross and started persecuting Christians.[31]

Simultaneously, the Western Roman Empire's expansion had not yet reached its climax. In the first three centuries A.D., Western Rome went on to conquer most of Europe, extending all the way to England. All of Spain was now completely under Roman control and its territory in Northern Africa expanded even further. During this expansion, imperial Rome experienced a transmittal, where the hegemony shifted from Roman polytheism to the Roman Catholic Church. However, did it really become a different hegemony—or remain the same one, just with a new image? As a hegemony is a dominant group who is influencing authority over others, all that we need to do is determine elements of Rome and the Catholic Church that are parallel in order to come to a conclusion.

So what are the elements of Catholicism? First and foremost,

---

[30] *The Middle East Under Rome,* by Maurice Sartre, pgs. 89-91 (Harvard University Press, 2005)
[31] *Mercer Dictionary of the Bible* edited by Watson Mills and Roger Bullard, pg. 668 (Mercer University Press, 1990)

Mary Hunt encapsulates its patriarchal nature:

> "The Male-only leadership model of the Roman Catholic
> Church renders the notion of women leaders moot. Only
> men can be ordained. Only ordained persons can make
> most decisions about sacraments, real estate, and church
> discipline. Thus women, even nuns, are excluded from
> leadership that involves decision making."[32]

The first popes claimed that slaves should be treated kindly, but they still believed in slavery as it was written into their dogma. When Rome was at its height in the late second and early third centuries A.D., we see what appears to be the complete transference of the hegemony's image. A Bishop named Hippolytus started shouting heresy at the current pope, Zephyrinusa, because this Pope believed that the trinity should not be personified, as it is metaphysical. Zephyrinus ended up dying and his deacon Callixtus became the Pope. Hippolytus along with other Bishops in Rome then split away from the Church, for they shouted heresy at Callixtus, just as they did to Zephyrinus. The Bishops that split away appointed Hippolytus as their new Pope.

Hippolytus then switched the day of Christ's birth to December 25th, the same day that the Roman Mithraic Mysteries celebrated the birth of the sun-god Mithras. This is rather ironic because the writings that Hippolytus left to us are the *Refutation of all Heresies,* which lists 33 Christian Gnostic systems as being heretical along with several pagan systems. Why would he switch Christ's birthday to a Roman (and originally Persian) pagan

---

[32] *Gender and Women's Leadership: A Reference, Volume 1* edited by Karen O'Connor, pg. 51 (SAGE, 2010)

holiday? On the other side, Pope Callixtus recognized a marriage between a Roman upper-class woman and a Christian slave as legal—but Hippolytus and the Bishops on his side disagreed with Callixstus' decision. Callixstus then either mysteriously died or was murdered. Hippolytus held his papacy (that split) for 18 years, and was later made a saint. This is where we see the paternal and state authority begin to become a major characteristic of the Catholic Church's hegemony.

Due to the beauty of critical thinking, it is rather easy to identify a paradox within this all. We already acknowledged what we can call "a real Christian": the Essenes, the Gnostics, and the Therapeuatae, as they were the ones who actually followed in the footsteps of Christ—they modeled their behavior on his. We cannot say the same thing about the majority of Catholics, however, for very blatant reasons. For the Roman Catholic Church, "A 'heretic' must be a Christian who challenges either the dogma of the Church or its policies, 'the formal denial or doubt of any defined doctrine of the Catholic faith.'"[33] This doesn't sound very "Christ-like," does it? The Roman Catholic Church then later deemed the Gnostics as heretics,[34] for they published too many Gospels describing their spiritual experiences, and these conflicted with the Church's authoritarian dogma. The Church also regarded the Essenes as heretics, claiming that "[...] the heresy was a combination of alien elements with Christian belief which threatened to submerge the Christian in the pagan."[35] Likewise, the Therapeutae became heretics for their ascetic, or hermit

---

[33] *Heresy in the Roman Catholic Church* by Michael Thomsett, pg. 1 (McFarland, 2011)
[34] Ibid, pg. 21
[35] *Colossians and Philemon* by Robert Wilson, pg. 39 (Continuum, 2005)

(hermetic) way of life.[36] From here we can identify the completing element in showing that the Roman hegemony was transferred into the Church: the Roman Empire persecuted the original Christians and the Roman Catholic Church also persecuted the original Christians.

The Roman Empire then began its fall and the Catholic Church its rise. The Catholic Church went on to burn cats because they thought that they were evil, which ended up creating an overpopulation of mice and rats, starting plagues. The Church vehemently burned heretics and status quo-threatening books as well, and they sent armies of children to go reclaim Jerusalem (as it was once in Roman control), and later slaughtered, enslaved, and colonized aboriginal peoples around the world—but so did the Protestants.

As such, what we are seeing is that this Piscean age has not been truly Christian—whether Protestant or Catholic (although the Lutheran movement was definitely an improvement in terms of walking in the footsteps of Christ). All of this implies that during this age, there have been authoritarian, materialistic, egotistic, and patriarchal archetypes that have been predominant in the psyches of many individuals, more so than the other archetypes. Before we look into these archetypes, we have to take a leap back in time, in order to paint a better image of what the archetypes even are.

When looking into the priesthood of ancient Egypt, we arrive at an image that is quite similar to that of the Essenes, the Gnostics, and the Therapeutae. Just like the Essenes, "In the

---

[36] *Encyclopedia of Catholicism* by Frank Flinn, pg. 461 (Infobase Publishing, 2007)

minds of the Egyptians the concepts of priest and purification through water were inseparable."[37] The priests of Heliopolis were known as the Great Seers and gave Moses his 'staff of Isis'; they taught astrology to Abraham and geometry to Joseph.[38] The priests also practiced celibacy, baptism, and circumcision.[39] The priests were required to be well-learned in medicine, covering anatomy, pathology, surgery, pharmacology, ophthalmology and gynecology—"All spheres of human inquiry were held to be interrelated and knowledge religious and scientific seemed to be one and inseparable."[40] Moreover, the priests actively lived a righteous life.

In *Volume 1* we learned that the "Heliopolian" system of the Egyptians saw the universe to be myriads of dualisms coming from a singular source. Due to this cosmological view, the feminine was regarded as highly as the masculine was. In effect, the opinions of the priests rubbed off onto the laypeople of Egypt, although lacking the priests' righteousness. Dr. Joann Fletcher writes,

"The Egyptians recognized female violence in all its forms, their queens even portrayed crushing their enemies, executing prisoners or firing arrows at male opponents as well as the non-royal women who stab and overpower invading soldiers. Although such scenes are often disregarded as illustrating 'fictional' or ritual events, the literary and archaeological evidence is less easy to dismiss. Royal women

---

[37] *Isis in the Ancient World* by R.E. Witt, pg. 89 (Johns Hopkins University Press, 1997)
[38] Ibid.
[39] Ibid, pgs. 90-1
[40] Ibid, pg. 50

undertake military campaigns whilst others are decorated for their active role in conflict. Women were regarded as sufficiently threatening to be listed as 'enemies of the state', and female graves containing weapons are found throughout the three millennia of Egyptian history."[41]

Fletcher goes on to explain that women were portrayed at every level of society as equals to men. He explains that a woman cargo-sailor yelled at a man "[...] get out of my way while I'm doing something important!" Women received equal pay rations as men for their work—royal women owned estates and workshops and controlled the treasury, and "[...] non-royal women as independent citizens could also own their own property, buy and sell it, make wills and even choose which of their children would inherit."[42]

It is well known that the Near East (and in particular, Egypt) influenced the formation of ancient Greece. During ancient Greece's beginning, Egypt was in contact with the Greeks and by the time the Hellenic period was at its culmination, Egypt's philosophy had affected the beliefs and culture of Greece immensely.[43] Although the Greeks transformed their deities into their own image, there was a transmigration of Egyptian deities and other cosmic deities of antiquity that held their prestige in Greece: Serapis being associated with Apollo and Asclepius; Neith with Athena; Bast with Artemis; Hathor with Dendera and

---

[41] See *Warrior Women to Female Pharaohs: Careers for Women in Ancient Egypt* by Dr. Joann Fletcher, at: http://www.bbc.co.uk/history/ancient/egyptians/women_01. shtml

[42] Ibid.

[43] *Ancient Greece: From Prehistoric to Hellenistic Times* by Thomas Martin, pg. 21 (Yale University Press, 2000)

Aphrodite; Isis with Artemis; Thoth with Hermes, and so on.[44] None struck more deep than Isis, however, as R.E. Witt shows that she appeared all throughout the Mediterranean (Northern Africa, Southern Europe, and Asia Minor), appearing as far north as London and York in Britannia and Rhine and Danube in Germania.[45] "Besides her identification with Aphrodite, Tyche, Nike, Hygieia (as at Epidaurus), and Artemis, she is also invoked as Astarte of Phoenicia, as the Mother of the Gods, and as the Great Mother."[46] Isis is the cause of righteousness to prevail, the reason parents should be loved by children and vice-versa, and the reason there is rebirth; she is arguably the most empowering deity for the feminine, as she made the power of women equal to men—held as one of the most important deities in ancient Egypt.

The priests and priestesses of Tithorea, in ancient Greece, exemplify both Egypt's influence and its prestige. Here a temple was built for the worship of Isis that only the priests and priestesses were allowed to enter. R.E. Witt writes that these Tithorean priests were only allowed to enter this temple when Isis summoned them via a dream.[47] Pausanias from the second century A.D. tells a story of a layman who disrespected this sacred oath and went into the temple. After entering, he found ghosts to be everywhere throughout the temple and ran home (to tell people what he saw) and dropped dead on the way back.[48]

---

[44] *Isis in the Ancient World* by R.E. Witt, pg. 54; 65; 67 (Johns Hopkins University Press, 1997)
[45] Ibid, pg. 56-7
[46] Ibid, pgs. 68-9
[47] Ibid, pg. 66

It is commonly believed that ancient Greece was highly patriarchal like Rome. However, new findings displayed at the Onassis Cultural Center that have been entitled "Worshiping Women: Ritual and Reality in Classical Athens," show that women played a huge role in Greek society. It is true that their role in Greece was distorted from Greece's prototype, Egypt, as women were no longer able to vote and had little to no decision in whom they could marry. Despite this, the feminine in ancient Greece was still held highly. Women played a huge role in religion and politics—"The priestess secures the peace."[49] The myths of ancient Greece perhaps typifies their role punctually. "Women are certainly not thin on the ground in Greek myth. Often they are accorded considerable prominence."[50] In fact, the Greek creation myth has the creation of both man and woman. [51] As such, what can be concluded is that as the cosmic religion of Egypt shifted into Greece, a distortion took place, but women were not yet completely degraded.

If Greece is a product of Egypt and Mesopotamia, then Rome is a product of Greece. As Greece associated its deities with Egypt's and Mesopotamia's, Rome associated its deities with

---

[48] *Description of Greece* by Pausanias, 10.32.16 at: http://perseus.uchicago.edu/perseus-cgi/citequery3.pl?dbname=GreekTexts&query=Paus.%2010.32.16&getid=1

[49] See *Liberating ancient Greek women from myth* by The Washington Times at: http://www.washingtontimes.com/news/2009/jan/07/its-a-womans-world/?page=all

[50] *Women in ancient Greece* by Sue Blundell, pg. 16 (Harvard University Press, 1995)

[51] *Hesiod: Works and Days and Theogony* translated by Stanley Lombardo, pgs. 61-90 (Hackett, 1993)

Greece's. Likewise, as the harmony of Egypt was distorted by Greece—with what we will term "minor-patriarchy" and the need to transform the deities into their own, personified images—Rome created an even bigger travesty out of the cosmic belief-system, by creating "complete-patriarchy." Professor McDonnel writes,

> "In ancient Rome, patriarchy, although unusually strong and enduring, was not the only hegemonic masculinity. It was precisely because of the peculiarly strong and enduring nature of Roman patriarchal power that an alternative form of manhood was not only fashioned, but institutionalized."[52]

As Rome's cosmology is still a distorted version of Egypt's, there still were goddesses in its pantheon; however, these goddesses were degraded from their original nature as the transmission into "complete-patriarchy" was enacted. This can be seen with the emperor Tiberius, who reigned during the days of Christ (14 B.C. to 37 A.D.). Tiberius didn't like it very much at all that citizens of Rome were worshipping Isis. So he burned down the Iseum temple, threw the statue of Isis into the Tigris river, and crucified all of the priests and priestesses.[53]

According to the "complete-patriarchy" established in Rome and wholly actualized with the Roman Catholic Church, the Western World in its recent timeline has been led to believe that there are only two primal models or archetypes: Jesus Christ and the Devil/Satan. Despite this narrow, patriarchal view, we still have the contrast of duality: light/dark or good/evil. However, as I

---

[52] *Roman Manliness: "Virtus" and the Roman Republic* by Myles McDonnell, pg. 173 (Cambridge University Press, 2006)
[53] *Religions of Rome; Volume 1* by Beard, North, and Price, pg. 231 (Cambridge University Press, 1998)

am constantly experiencing a much more complicated state of being, this approach is rather lame—it is lacking of its true substance. As in one moment I may experience the fatherly wisdom pour into my awareness; or in another feel the motherly understanding take control of my psyche; or in another moment feel darkness control my mood, I don't believe that the Christ-Satan duality really sums up my state of being—our states of being.

It is much more valid to assume that there are far more archetypes within the psyches of humankind that are accessible for the microcosm-to-macrocosm relationship, far more archaic archetypes that weren't so recently designated. More importantly, these archetypes aren't only masculine. When studying the religions of ancient civilizations, the Eastern religions, the shamanic tribal philosophies, and even the beliefs of the original Christians, it is quite clear that these peoples—who were so closely connected to nature—held this same understanding.

Throughout the ancient world, if one worshiped a certain god or goddess, then they were worshipping this archetype within themselves. Their aim was to become "as like" as possible to this archetype. However, not only did they worship this archetype within themselves, but they also worshipped it without themselves, as everything is within and without the microcosm. Thus, temples were constructed for the exterior worship of these archetypes that are within the macrocosm; and the true temple, the human body, was the worship place for the archetypes within the microcosm. Furthermore, the people of ancient cultures did not limit their worship to merely one archetype. In many cases all of the different archetypes of the local pantheon were embodied. An invocation directed towards a medicinal herb from the Paris

Papyrus demonstrates this harmonization,

> "Thou wast sown by Cronos, picked by Hera, preserved by
> Ammon, begotten by Isis, nourished by rain-giving Zeus; thou
> has grown thanks to the Sun and the dew. *Thou are the dew
> of all the gods, the heart of Hermes*, the seed of the first gods,
> the eye of the sun, the light of the moon, the dignity of Osiris,
> the beauty and splendor of heaven, etc. . . . As thou raisedst
> up Osiris, arise thyself! Rise as the Sun! Thy grandeur is as
> high as its zenith; thy roots are as deep as the abyss, etc. . . .
> Thy branches are the bones of Minerva; thy flowers the eye
> of Horus; thy seeds the seed of Pan, etc. . . .; I follow Hermes.
> I pluck thee with good fortune, the Good Spirit, at the lucky
> hour, on the day that is right and suitable for all things."
> (italics are mine)[54]

To attempt to understand the ancients, one must first attempt to
embody the archetypes into his or her psyche.

War or fighting deities show up everywhere. Furthermore,
these deities are not always masculine. To list several war
goddesses: Athena in Greece; Freyja in Norse mythology; Korrawi
from the Tamils' mythology (South Asia); Agasaya from
Mesopotamia; Anahita in Persian/Chaldean mythology, Oya and
Ifri from Africa; Chamunda, Kali, Matrikas, Kathyayini, etc. in
Hinduism, Andraste in Celtic mythology; the Slavonic goddess
Zroya; Pele in Hawaiian mythology; Qamaits in the mythology of
the Nuxálk peoples of North America; and Shaushka of the
Hittites. As both female and male war deities show up abundantly
everywhere, the "warriorship" archetype provides a suitable place

---

[54] *Patterns in Comparative Religion* by Mircea Eliade, pg. 297
(University of Nebraska Press, 1996)

to start in identifying the nature of the archetypes as a whole.

So what would define a war archetype? Well, first of all, its mundane understanding is inadequate. As archetypes are, in many ways, mythological, one must take a mythological approach to understand their nature. When doing so, one comes to understand that the mythologies embedded with the war archetype are symbolic. This symbolism is why a mundane approach will not arrive at a complete understanding—as one will make assumptions without proper contemplation. As such, a war archetype is most certainly not restricted to our mundane concept of "war." A war can be much deeper than a nation and its desire for power over another nation or nations—as a war can be going on inside of oneself, without oneself, between ideologies (good and evil) and so on. Thus, the war deities characterize an archetype within one's psyche that fights for what it believes in, fights for life, fights for love, and so on; or quite the contrary, fights for destruction, satisfaction—darkness. As we have seen with the case of Jesus, Balinas, etc., this archetype is most completely embodied when the individual fighting for what they believe in has a non-violent and non-militant approach. One does not need to kill or oppress to fight for his or her vision to manifest, but one certainly must 'fight' (or challenge others) for what they believe in to make it actualized.

Now that the symbolic nature of mythologies signifying particular archetypes has been presented, we can move on to the next example. In all areas where we find a definite form of writing (rather than a "petroglyphical" form) there are deities or legendary figures that are held as the source of this writing. In *Volume 1*, we saw that Wôdan from Scandinavia, Thoth from Egypt and Hermes from Greece were held to have brought writing to their regions. In China both a legendary hero/deity named Fúxī and Wenchang Dijun play this role; Saraswati and Ganesha in India, Ba'alat from Phoenicia, Tenjin in Japan, Nabu in Mesopotamia, and so forth, did as well. To understand the symbolism behind these writing deities, we are led back to: "everything is within and without the microcosm." The writing archetype is not defined as the microcosm since it is something higher than our current level of existence; but the microcosm *can be* defined by the writing archetype (along with other archetypes). It then follows that the reason that these mythologies are very similar is that they retell an archaic event that took place within the psyches of humankind. The deities, alone, did not bring writing to humanity; instead they relied upon human microcosms to bring writing. An epiphany that occurred within a person or multiple people was triggered by the writing archetype within the microcosm, and this event is what conveyed writing to the macrocosm.

The words of Jung bring this into perspective.

"[One's] hand is seized, [one's] pen writes things that his (or her) mind contemplates with amazement. The work brings with it its own form; anything [that one] wants to add is rejected, and what he himself (or she herself) would like to reject is thrust back at him (or her). While his (or her) conscious mind stands amazed and empty before this phenomenon, he (or she) is overwhelmed by a flood of thoughts and images which he (or she) never intended to create and which his (or her) own will could never have brought into being. Yet in spite of [oneself] he (or she) is forced to admit that it is his (or her) own self speaking, his (or her) own inner nature revealing itself and uttering things which he (or she) would never have entrusted to his (or her) tongue. He (or she) can only obey the apparently alien impulse within him (or her) and follow where it leads, sensing that [one's] work is greater than [oneself], and wields a power which is not his (or hers) and which he (or she) cannot command. Here the artist is not identical with the process of creation; [one] is aware that [one] is subordinate to his (or her) work or stands outside it, as though he (or she) were a second person; or as though a person other than [oneself] had fallen within the magic circle of an alien will." (parenthesis are mine)[55]

This phenomenon that Jung beautifully sums up is synonymous with how writing was first established in civilizations. An epiphany that seemed to come from something higher enabled the discovery of writing, but it could not do so without the free-willed cooperation of a microcosm or multiple microcosms. Furthermore, his assertion denotes that the writing archetype guided him in his work.

For the sake of avoiding redundancy, we will not go on to list all of the other deities from around the world and how they all appear to epitomize the same archetype. Instead we will just briefly list what they epitomize in order to get a more detailed idea of the archetypes: motherly nurturing, agricultural/botanical abilities, wisdom, metallurgical abilities, craftsmanship, masonry, music, magic, critical thinking, city-planning, mischief, "warriorship," healing or curative abilities, oracular abilities, linguistics, hunting, sexual abilities, beauty, justice, and so on. On all continents there are also elemental archetypes: formers or

---

[55] *The Portable Jung* by Carl Jung, pg. 311 (The Viking Press, 1974)

guardians of mountains, foothills, rivers, valleys, jungles, forests, the sky, the ocean, fire, water, air, earth, and so on, as well as archetypes of plants, trees, and animals.

As there will be readers who have their heads submerged in the status quo, I must elaborate on the elemental archetypes further, in order for these "status quoians' " interest to not dissipate.

Baby rattlesnakes are abandoned immediately at birth. They do not have a parent figure or figures that teach them how to be a rattlesnake. Yet, they all end up being rattlesnakes. They all hunt in the same way—using their rattles to invoke fear amongst their prey. They all seem to know that deserts and prairies with an abundance of rocks is their ideal ecological habitat, as the rocks provide a hiding place to call home. They all know that spring and fall is when they should mate. They all know that when winter comes along, they need to find a location where they can hibernate in safety. As rattlesnakes are abandoned at birth and do not have a parental model, they are a suitable example for elemental archetypes. If rattlesnakes do not have archetypes that guide their psyches, then how else do they intuitively know how to do all of these things that define them as rattlesnakes?

Again, the Director of the Yggdrasil Wildlife Center, Lila Travis, tells a story of abandoned baby fawns that hints of archetypes.[56] A couple ended up becoming the caretakers of two baby fawns. These fawns were abandoned by their mothers (who were both most likely first-time parents). This couple then raised the fawns, which came to believe that the human caretakers were now their

---

[56] *Fawn Stories* by Lila Travis; at:
http://yuwr.org/stories/fawn-stories/

mothers. As fawns rely on a very tightly knitted relationship with their mothers, the caretakers had to be attentive in raising them. After two months of care, the fawns were gradually integrated back into the wild. Soon the fawns became independent enough and permanently lived in the wild again. After being monitored weekly, the researchers found that these human-raised fawns were not lonesome wanderers out in the wild. Instead, they joined herds of deer, as they would have done if they were raised by actual deer. Despite isolation from their species during adolescence, the fawns became a part of their species nearly instantaneously during the reintroduction back into the wild.

On a more obscure level, let's look into the whole geographical nature of our planet. It is very difficult to envision a different structure for our planet for its carbon-hydrogen-oxygen based life. As mountains breach the highest land elevations, they tend to have cold enough winters so that snow falls and builds up. As the seasons cycle, the snow melts in these mountain areas, and because of the elevation, the melted snow is pulled to lower elevations due to gravity. This newly melted water ventures its way into rivers, which then travels into even the most arid climates—providing water for life to continue—until it reaches the sea. During this adventure, water that is "used" will eventually experience condensation. After condensation into storm fronts in the atmosphere, this water will eventually precipitate—raining/snowing back down on to Earth, starting the process all over again. This whole process is mimicked within our own microcosms. Our mountains (the heart) pumps blood through our rivers (arteries) until it is deoxidized and then makes it way to our clouds (veins), making its way back to the mountain (the heart), all so that our life goes on.

Or why is it that the veins in leaves resemble the same geometries of the veins in humans? Or that a brain cell looks like our universe? The ingenuity behind the elemental forces of life certainly appear to be archetypal in nature.

2 THE OLD WORLD

"Among the things that are part of the substance of the psychic are psychoid archetypes. The characteristic that is peculiar to the archetype is that it manifests itself not only psychically-subjectively but also physically-objectively; in other words, it is possible that it can be proved to be both a psychic inner occurrence and also a physical external one. I regard this phenomenon as an indication of the fact that the physical and psychic matrix is identical."
– Carl Jung to Wolfgang Pauli[57]

I must first note that the Old World and the New World have been switched for this study. The New World will be in reference to Europe, Asia, Arabia, and only the Northern part of Africa. These are the areas in recent history where "historic civilization" has developed (along with Mexico and Peru/Ecuador in the Americas). However, in each of the histories of these regions, we

---

[57] *Atom and Archetype: The Pauli/Jung Letters, 1932-1958* by Wolfgang Pauli and Carl Jung, pg. 126 (Princeton University Press, 2001)

are able to discern that a tribal way of life was at its foundation, i.e. Twelve Tribes of Israel, Ten Tribes of China, etc. Thus, the Old World will be in reference to the American, Australian, and African First Peoples. As a tribal way of life is far more resembling of our most distant ancestors of humanoids, it deserves the title of "old." As these tribal cultures are all very similar, they resemble the primal human still living in the garden.

Before venturing into the mythologies of the Old World, we must establish a pattern that is congruent between these continents. In these regions, the heroes in the mythologies are nearly always described anthropomorphically—the human hero is described as some type of animal or even plant or tree.

As the primal peoples needed only the garden for their prosperity, their philosophies understand human's connection to all other life. In Darwinian terms, it is understood that everything is derived from a single form of life on Earth that has gradually been mutating and evolving. The primal peoples projected this in their culture. It appears as if the animal motif in their mythologies is describing the personality of the human protagonist using the personality of a specific animal to metaphorically characterize it— as if the animals and different life systems are connected within our being. A rabbit is quick, witty, tranquil, and so on; a cat is playful and is a hunter; a mountain goat climbs the highest heights, overcoming the most difficult terrain; obsidian stone is tough and a bringer of technology; a medicinal herb is predictable, cleansing, and curative in nature, and so forth. All of the personalities of various life systems and elements on this planet—or what characterizes them—are possible traits or personalities that can define a specific human.

In the myths of the Algonquin peoples, who inhabited all of

the area around the Great Lakes in North America, stories have survived of the "Giant Rabbit." Like Jesus Christ, this rabbit comes in the guise of the primal Creator, or singular source, and is described as a manifestation of light. The rabbit brings the skills of fishing and hunting, religious rites, "petroglyphical" writing, interpretation of dreams, and so on to the humans.[58] This heroic figure reveals these to humans by observing nature. For example, "Having closely studied how the spider spreads her web to catch flies, he invented the art of knitting nets for fishing, and taught it to his descendants."[59] The rabbit is quick, witty, and peaceful, and the Great Rabbit is also.

An equipollent shows up in the tribes in the Wabanaki Confederacy, with their culture hero, Glooskap. "He taught them to build villages and sail canoes; to hunt and fish and plant corn; to bury fish in their fields [so] that the corn might grow. All that they knew, they learned [from] him."[60] Glooskap is quite similar to the heroes established in Chapter One in several ways: one, he comes from the East—from the rising sun; two, he ascends to the heaven in his white canoe after he taught the people what they needed to know;[61] three, he is challenged by his "twin brother," Maslum, his equal, but a manifestation of darkness that undermines what would have been paradise on Earth from Glooskap's exertion.

The tale of Glooskap illustrates themes that show up with the

---

58 *American Hero-Myths* by Daniel Brinton, pg. 38 (H.C. Watts & Co., 1882)
59 Ibid, pg. 39
60 *Indian Hero Tales* by Gilbert Livingstone Wilson, pg. 15 (American Book Company, 1818)
61 *Oxford Companion to World Mythology* by David Leeming, pg. 152 (Oxford University Press, 2005)

more contemporary cultural heroes. He defeats his evil brother (an equivalent of Satan, Mara, etc.), but loses in the end, in the sense that paradise on Earth was not achieved. He tricks a witch that is trying to poison him to death, and is triumphant over her. And he completes several other similar 'quests.' He is light combating dark.

We have already seen that Quetzalcoatl and his deviants came from the East, as he represents light.[62] Quetzalcoatl brought technology, magic, religion, etc. to the humans. He also has a twin brother who signifies darkness: Xolotl. The clash between Xolotl and Quetzalcoatl is mirrored in the Glooskap story.

For the Warlpiri peoples of Northern Australia, no myth rings as deeply throughout the people than the story of the *jajirdi*, or the spotted cat. The story starts off with the spotted cat running to many villages to warn the people living there that an evil beast is destroying everything that comes in its proximity. But the spotted cat is not truly a cat, but a heroic man who has the mythical power of shape-shifting, or becoming whichever animal or insect he wants to become. The hero is worried that the beast has already devoured his children and his fellow tribe's folk. As he runs up to each area, he tells the people not to light a fire, for the beast will see the fire's radiance. He also instructs everyone not to hunt—to just eat plants and bugs in the grass until the beast's devastation has ended—and to be quiet and not talk. When he gets to his family he explains to them that:

> "[The beast] has carried around the bodies of children hanging from its armbands, and the bodies of older boys hanging from its belt. It has also carried around many bodies

---

[62] See the Afterword of *Volume 1*

of fully-grown adults, and also tiny babies. It is a terrible man-eater. At present it is near here to the east at Warlaku, at the water there, which is flowing, like a river."[63]

From the context of the story the beast appears to be a mythical giant.

After warning many different tribes about this beast, the spotted cat goes to find it and defeat it. He doesn't know which animal he wants to change into to carry out this task. He asks himself if he should change into a hornet but decides that the beast would 'brush that off quickly.' Then he wonders whether an ant would be his best option, but the beast could easily crush an ant. He goes on contemplating all of his options.

When the spotted cat gets close to the beast, he sharpens his wooden spears and hides them in the grass nearby. He finally decides to change into a stinging ant and conceals himself near the water where the beast drinks. When the beast approaches, the stinging ant jumps onto his lips and stings repetitively. He then jumps off while the beast is confused. "It bent down again towards the water. It had the big stones it used with the club. It bent down to the water again. He stung it again, a little later. It took up a stone and started beating itself severely. Yes, it beat itself."[64] As the giant was very thirsty, he kept trying to drink water and the stinging ant continued to bite him in different places. The beast reacts in the same way and starts beating itself to the point of mutilation. The hero then turns back into a man, grabs his spears that he hid earlier, and spears the giant straight through the body.

---

[63] *Warlpiri Dreamings and Histories* by Peggy Napaljarri and Lee Cataldi, pg. 5 (HarperCollins, 1994)
[64] Ibid, pg. 15

The hero returns to the villages, spreading the news that the beast has been slain. "He returned to his home forever, and there forever he went in."[65]

The Mwindo Epic, derived from the Nyanga Peoples of the Congo River area in Africa, is a story that mirrors Perseus' tale in Greek mythology, as we will see in the next chapter.[66] [67] However, its rhetoric possesses the same shamanic symbolism as the tales from the other areas in what I have termed the "Old World." The King in the village of Tubondo, Shemmwindo, sleeps with seven women one night and impregnates all of them. Six of the women birth daughters all on the same day. His seventh wife, Nyamwindo, remains pregnant and the abnormally long gestation period begins to alarm some of the tribe's people. Suddenly supernatural events begin to occur, such as firewood manifesting at her door already cut and water vessels filling themselves. She then births the protagonist, Mwindo, who is born already able to talk and walk—it is a supernatural birth, for Mwindo is not an ordinary man.

Shemwindo fears his son for this reason, and aims to kill him. He throws several spears into the hut that Mwindo is in, but Mwindo stops the spears using the magical powers of his voice. After more failed attempts to kill his son, Shemwindo then orders Nyamwindo to put him into a wooden drum and seal it with animal skin. She does so and throws her son into the river.

---

[65] Ibid, pg. 19
[66] *Oral Epics from Africa* edited by John Johnson, Thomas Hale, and Stephen Belcher, pgs. 285-93 (Indian University Press, 1997)
[67] *The Hero With an African Face: Mythic Wisdom of Traditional Africa* by Clyde W. Ford (Bantam Books, 1999)

From here Mwindo goes through many struggles, tests, and adventures. After breaking free from his imprisonment in the drum, his dogs are starving, and using his magical scepter (that he was born clutching) he creates food out of thin air to feed them. Mwindo then counsels with the deities of the Netherworld, receiving the courage and heroism that he needs to carry out his destiny. He is then guided by animal spirits to retrieve honey from a tree: Spider and Bat. Spider gives him rope and Bat gives him nails to climb the *mpaki* tree, which is the symbol of the Cosmic Axis. Mwindo then climbs the cosmic tree, but gets terrified up in the sky. He calls upon the spirit of Lightning to aid him in his struggles. Lighting strikes the tree and knocks the honey down.

Mwindo goes into the forest to hunt for a pig, and encounters a dragon. This beast is described as being terrifying and black—it has sharp teeth and the tail of an eagle. Mwindo slays the dragon, and is then heralded among the people. His father, out of shame, resigns his title as the king and appoints Mwindo to be the ruler. From here Mwindo is guided by the sun, moon, and stars—gods— to bring just laws to the people and be a righteous sovereign.

3 THE NEW WORLD

"Every myth, whatever its nature, recounts an event that took place in illo tempore (in that time), and constitutes as a result, a precedent and pattern for all the actions and "situations" later to repeat that event. Every ritual, and every meaningful act that [a human] performs, repeats a mythical archetype; and, as we saw, this repetition involves the abolition of profane time and placing of [the human] in magico-religious time which has no connection with succession in the true sense, but forms the "eternal now" of mythical time." - Mircea Eliade[68]

The heroic stories from Northern Europe are filled with reoccurring themes. In the story of Sigurd and the Nibelungs, which is told in three different tales from the Icelandic/Germanic heathendom—the *Nibelungen Lied*, *Thidreks Saga*, and the *Edda*—we have, perhaps, the best glimpse of this theme. The hero, Sigurd, explains, "I came a motherless child; I have no father

---

[68] *Patterns in Comparative Religion* by Mircea Eliade, pgs. 429-30 (University of Nebraska Press, 1996)

like the sons of men."[69] This supernatural birth of Sigurd is common throughout other heroic tales from the Icelandic/Germanic heathendom, such as the stories of Sigmund and Sinfjötli. All three of these heroes are born of "supernatural" birth—filled with suffering—who then rose to their destiny and slayed a dragon that was guarding a treasure and each story includes the act of vengeance. Furthermore, in each different tale, only the hero could wield the sword that was used to kill the dragon.

Only the hero possesses within him or herself the initiatory power or requirements to overcome the obstacle. In Sigurd's case, one of his "requirements" is characterized as "[...] the one who knows no fear."[70] This thought-modality is fundamental for the hero; however, the removal of fear is not necessarily an instantaneous acquirement or something that is *a priori* since conception. For the student of esotericism, the removal of fear will most likely be a process that first requires a certain psychological state to be activated.

Another of Sigurd's "requirements" was his heightened state of consciousness—or capability to work in the supernatural realms. This is because Sigurd has the ability to understand the language of birds. He makes fidelity with the bird kingdom, and then has birds guide him to a sleeping Valkyrie—a female spiritual being—the same thing as a faërie.[71] After waking up the Valkyrie, "She then becomes Sigurd's guardian and protectress and the source of his wisdom, as she speaks the runes and counsels which

---

[69] *The Edda: II. The Heroic Mythology of the North* by Winifred Faraday, pg. 15 (David Nutt, 1902)
[70] Ibid, pg. 20
[71] Ibid, pg. 19

are to help him in all difficulties."[72] It would be valid to say that this connection with higher consciousness is a requirement for the hero, as we shall see with the following cases.

In ancient Greece, this same pattern occurs in the heroic story of Perseus. The story begins with King Acrisius of Argos and his daughter Danaë. Acrisius went to Delphi to ask a priestess if he would ever have a boy, as he was looking for a son to carry on his dynasty. Instead of good news, the diviner reveals that Danaë will birth a son who will kill him. So to prevent this from occurring, Acrisius keeps Danaë locked up in a bronze room enclosed on all sides in aims to prevent her from getting pregnant. The Classicist Edith Hamilton explains what happens next:

> "As she sat there through the long days and hours with nothing to do, nothing to see except the clouds moving by overhead, a mysterious thing happened, a shower of gold fell from the sky and filled her chamber. How it was revealed to her that it was Zeus who had visited her in this shape we are not told, but she knew that the child she bore was his son."[73]

Once again, we have the "supernatural" birth of the hero. After Danaë gives birth to Perseus, Acrisius finds out; infuriated, he sends Danaë and her child out into the ocean imprisoned in a floating chest. They get directed along the ocean's current until they wash up upon the shore of an island in a way that underlies a destiny to their lives. A fishermen named Dictys finds them and helps them get out of the chest. Dictys and his wife then raise Danaë and Perseus as if they were their own kids.

Several years later, when Perseus is now a young man, Dictys'

---

[72] Ibid, pg. 21
[73] *Mythology* by Edith Hamilton, pg. 142 (Mentor, 1969)

brother, Polydectes, the cruel king of the island, convinces him to slay one of the heads off the Gorgons (i.e. Medusa is one of the three Gorgons—serpentine mythical beings), for Polydectes is secretly in love with Danaë and needs Perseus out of the way to pursue his romance. Perseus, young and naïve, then leaves to go retrieve Medusa's head—a task everyone else thought was suicide. But, like Sigurd and the other Scandinavian heroes, Perseus is not without help. Hermes and Athena come to his aid. Hermes gives him a magical sword, and then tells him that he must make allegiance with the nymphs of the North before he attempts to slay Medusa. The nymphs are female spiritual beings—the same thing as faëries or Valkyries. Athena then gives Perseus her shiny bronze shield, and tells him that he must use it to see, for if he looked directly into any of the Gorgons' eyes, he would turn to stone. When Perseus finally makes it to the nymphs, he notices that they are very kind and majestic beings. They then give Perseus three magical items: winged sandals that allowed him to fly, a wallet that could carry any object regardless of size, and an invisibility cap.

Perseus is now ready to take on the Gorgons. After a long adventure, Perseus makes it to the Gorgons—following the advice of Hermes and Athena—he shields his vision from direct eye contact. Edith Hamilton describes the Gorgons that Perseus saw reflected in the shield as: "Creatures with great wings and bodies covered with golden scales and hair [of] mass made of twisting snakes."[74] This description sounds rather similar to a dragon. Perseus was then guided by Athena and Hermes for every following step—and triumphantly, Athena guides Perseus' hand as he decapitates Medusa.

---

[74] Ibid, pg. 146

For the present study, we will not look in much depth into what happened to Perseus after this feat. In brief summary, after more heroic adventures, he does end up killing his grandfather, King Acricius, as the prophecy declared—although unintentionally—and once again we have the theme of vengeance.

Far off in the land of China this same pattern shows up in *Sōushénjì,* a 4th century A.D. compilation of legends and tales on the topic of communicating with spirits. *Sōushénjì* is entitled "In Search of the Supernatural" in English, and one of the tales tells the story of Li Chi.[75] In this case, we have a heroine. Li Chi, the youngest of six daughters, disregards her parent's authority and heads out to slay a dragon that has already taken the life of nine different individuals who had attempted to end its wrath. Li Chi is smart about her approach, however, and brings the sharpest sword she can find and a serpent-hunting dog. She brings balls of sweet rice and places these near the entrance of the cave. The smell of the sweet rice lures the dragon out of its cave, upon which the dog clamps into it. Li Chi then jumps out of hiding and slashes the dragon several times. The wounds struck deep, ultimately killing the dragon. She goes into the cave, grabs the nine skulls of those whom the dragon had already killed, and thinks, "Their timidity brought them here, my boldness kept me here." Because of this vengeance, the King of Yueh makes Li Chi his queen.

A couple thousand miles across the East China Sea, we find the same pattern in Japan. The Kojiki (The Record of Ancient

---

[75] *In Search of the Supernatural* by Bao Gan, translated by Kenneth DeWoskin and J.I. Crump Jr., pgs. 230-1 (Stanford University Press, 1996)

Matters) dates from the early 8th century A.D. and it chronicles verbal stories that have been told in Japan from times immemorial. Sosa no wo no Mikoto is the protagonist, and the plotline is centered on his soon-to-be maiden, Kushinadahime, the last of eight daughters who have been devoured by a dragon. This dragon is holding Kushinadahime captive and she faces a similar situation as her sisters. However, unlike her dead sisters, Kushinadahime is a *miko*, one who serves a deity or multiple deities. Similarly, Sosa no wo no Mikoto, the hero, is of supernatural birth but was forced to return to Earth for his disruptive actions.[76] Thus he embodies the heroic archetype in aims to get back to heaven. The dragon is red-eyed, and it has eight tails and eight heads—it represents dread and darkness.[77]

Sosa no wo no Mikoto implements a strategic approach like Li Chi did in China, and gets the dragon drunk with sake. The dragon falls into slumber and Sosa no wo no Mikoto chops it into pieces with his sword. After doing so, he examines the inside of the dragon and finds a "divine" sword. He recognizes that he must give this back to the heavens. After saving Kushinadahime he then marries her and they have a child.

In (former) Yugoslavia, stories were told of Yuk the "Dragon Despot." Yuk is also born of a supernatural birth, in which some accounts describe him as being born with wolf's hair, blue flames blazing out his mouth and nose, and red skin.[78] A dragon living in the Jastrebac mountains in Serbia is devastating the lands and this

---

[76] *The Cambridge History of Japan, Volume 1* edited by Delmer Brown, pg. 466 (Cambridge University Press, 1993)
[77] *Nihongi: Chronicles of Japan from the Earliest Times to A.D. 697, Volume 1* (Society, 1896)
[78] *The Growth of Literature* by H. Munro Chadwick and Nora Chadwick, pg. 322 (Cambridge University Press, 2010)

dragon fears only one person, Yuk. Yuk, being the hero, soars up to where the dragon is flying, clubs his wings and then decapitates the dragon. This set of myths is also filled with spiritual beings name *Vila*. Mircea Eliade explains,

> "Fairies (*Vila*) cure wounded heroes, resuscitate them, foretell the future to them, warn them of imminent dangers, just as in myth a female being aids and protects the hero. No heroic 'ordeal' is omitted: [Yuk shoots] an arrow through an apple, [jumps] over several horses, [recognizes] a girl among a group of youths dressed alike, and so on."[79]

Once again, we have the pattern of guidance by spiritual beings.

In Persian mythology, we are told of the story of Rostam. A dragon is hiding in the darkness,

> "[...] described as resembling a black mountain which blots out the sun and the moon. The beast's eyes are said to be like two shining pools of blood, and fire bursts out of its mouth which, when open, looks like a deep dark cave."[80]

With many of the characters in this story being humans, Rostam is one who is guided by supernatural forces and he slays the dragon. Again, this is paralleled in another Persian story from the *Shahnama of Shah Tahmasp*. Isfandiyar is the protagonist who uses his wit like the other heroes. He builds a box with sharp spikes on it, which the dragon swallows. Isfandiyar is hiding in the box, and then puts his sword through the dragon's head, killing it.

---

[79] *Cosmos and History* by Mircea Eliade, pg. 41 (Harper & Row, 1959)
[80] *World of Myths: Volume Two* edited by Marina Warner and Felipe Fernandez-Armesto, pg. 128 (University of Texas Press, 2004)

Some scholars have argued that these dragon-slaying stories are derived from one common prototype in antiquity. We will not refute this theory, but contemplate an alternative interpretation where these stories hint of an archetypal force that has been influencing the psyches of various cultures in their respective geographical locations.

The common prototype concept is deficient for this reason: not only does the dragon motif show up throughout Asia, Europe, Asia Minor and Africa, but in America and Australia we find stories that embody the same dragon-like character, i.e. the "beast," Maslum or Xolotl. If we then continue with the theory that these stories are derived from a common ancestor story, then we are left with an anomaly. The story shows up on every continent inhabited by human life—continents which are isolated from each other geographically. In the case of Australia, *homo sapiens* migrated to the continent as far back as 50,000 years ago.[81] According to the theory, the myth would have had to arrive at the same time and then survive up until the present. Through critical thinking, this devalues the creditability of the theory.

What adheres to logic and reason is that these stories do indeed have a common prototype. But, this prototype is not the same story being told for well over 50,000 years and has mutated in each culture slightly. Instead, an archetype within the psyches of humans has reproduced this story. However, this does not mean that the heroic story did not actually repeat itself in history. The myth's ability to survive through many generations implies

---

[81] "New ages for human occupation and climatic change at Lake Mungo, Australia" by Bowler, Johnston, Olley, Prescott, Roberts, Shawcross, and Spooner, pgs. 837-40 in the journal *Nature* (February, 2003)

that a human in each culture really did embody this archetype and defeat the dragon, the beast, or "the evil one," and this archetype then guided others to keep the story alive through mythology.

With this established, we must seek out an esoteric understanding of the common tale. In *Volume 1*, we learned that to understand something esoterically, we must interpret the symbol or symbols that surround it.

The dragon is clearly a symbol, unless we believe that there really were dragons during these times. This is a possibility, as we have unearthed many skeletons of dinosaurs, some of which seem to mimic the description of these dragons. However, dinosaurs are held to have disappeared 66-million years ago, making this theory unlikely. Thus, the dragon in mythology, and dinosaurs on earth, are both symbols for an archetype.

What does the dragon symbolize in each myth? It is described as vile looking; the dragon is devastating the area, killing anything that comes in its proximity—it is blood thirsty, killing innocent life not for survival but for satisfaction. It is also guarding a treasure, the treasure of peace and prosperity. These are only achieved after the hero slays the dragon. This is exactly what the beast in the *jajirdi* myth of the Warlpiri people of Australia symbolizes. It is what is holding humanity back from living a better standard of life.

What other symbols are recurring throughout these tales? The hero is either a teenager or a young man or woman. Higher forms of consciousness guide the hero—he or she works within the metaphysical realms in order to accomplish his or her task. Furthermore, destiny is inherent in all of the tales.

PART TWO

Pathos

4 EÄ

"All that is gold does not glitter,
Not all those who wander are lost;
The old that is strong does not wither,
Deep roots are not reached by the frost.
From the ashes a fire shall be woken,
A light from the shadows shall spring;
Renewed shall be blade that was broken,
The crownless again shall be king."
J.R.R Tolkien[82]

To establish that archetypal forces have guided certain individuals to keep the myth alive (in a modern, fictional fashion), the cases must have significant success, while still embodying the archetypal patterns discussed in Part One. Furthermore, due to the archetypal guidance, we should also find esoteric information and metaphysical cues embedded in the works of these individuals.

The Lord of the Rings and *The Hobbit*, as of the publication date of this volume, have sold an estimated 250 million copies

---

[82] *The Lord of the Rings: The Fellowship of the Ring* by J.R.R. Tolkien, pg. 212 (Ballantine Books)

combined. The *Harry Potter* series has been even more successful, selling a total of 450 million copies between all seven books, making it the best-selling book series in history. Tolkien was to both youth and adults during the middle-20th century as Rowling is to both youth and adults of the beginning of this 21st century. With the motion picture films of these stories, many people who haven't read the books are also familiar with their plotlines. Due to this success, the works of J.R.R. Tolkien and J.K. Rowling shall be used in metaphorically explaining the archetypes.

At Oxford University, Tolkien taught courses ranging from English and Germanic philology, Old English heroic verse, the history of English, studies on various old English and Middle English texts, Gothic, Old Icelandic and Medieval Welsh.[83] Tolkien was well-versed in the mythologies from Europe and these mythologies activated a level of awareness inside his genius.

In an essay entitled "Tree and Leaf: On Fairy Stories" originally published by Oxford University Press in 1947, Tolkien explains the foundation of the themes in his fiction stories:

"It is too narrow, even if we reject the diminutive size, for fairy-stories are not in normal English usage stories *about* fairies or elves, but stories about Fairy, that is *Faërie,* the realm or state in which fairies have their beginning. *Faërie* contains many things besides elves and fays, and besides dwarfs, witches, trolls, giants, or dragons: it holds the seas, the moon, the sky; and the earth, and all things that are in it:

---

[83] *The Letters of J.R.R. Tolkien* by J.R.R. Tolkien, pg. 12 (George Allen & Unwin Publishers Ltd., 1981)

tree and bird, water and stone, wine and bread, and ourselves, mortal men, when we are enchanted."[84]

Tolkien implies that *Faërie* is a metaphysical realm that he was "enchanted" into glimpsing. It follows that his creativity for his novels was influenced by his enchantments.

Before dissecting the esoteric symbolism in the heroic stories of *The Lord of the Rings* and potentially grasping its meaning, we must first understand the cosmology of Tolkien's Middle-Earth and its universe, Eä. This cosmology was first figured out in 1917 before *The Hobbit* and *The Lord of the Rings* were written, and was constantly being worked on by Tolkien up until his death. Following his death, in 1977, Tolkien's son, Christopher, published this cosmology under the title *The Simarillion*.

According to this cosmology, before the universe manifest, there was the (personified) One, Eru Ilúvatar.

"He made first the Ainur, the Holy Ones, that were the offspring of his thought, and they were with him before aught else was made. And he spoke to them, propounding to them themes of music; and they sang before him."[85]

The themes of music that they follow are archetypal, made from the 'Flame Imperishable,' or the matrix of spirit. Ilúvatar orchestrates these archetypes to guide the Ainur, to play in harmony together, 'a Great Music.' The Ainur are also in dualities of male and female and are free to do as they please—they have

---

[84] *The Tolkien Reader* by J.R.R. Tolkien, pg. 9 (Ballantine Books Inc., 1966)
[85] *The Simarillion* by J.R.R. Tolkien, pg. 3 (Ballantine Books Inc., 1982)

both destiny and freedom. As such, this universe, in Tolkien's view, was a very long song—the one (uni) verse created multi-verses of male-female, free to create as they please.

This appears a fitting analogy of our own universe. A song is different mediums (or just one medium) creating vibrations in harmony as a whole. The sounds that come from this song are a form of energy that travels in an oscillating wave transmitted through a solid, liquid or gas. Each sound is different to the ear due to the nature of its wave. If it has a quickly oscillating wavelength then it has a high pitch, and vice versa. The foundation of matter in our universe is held together by vibrating wave-particle strings.[86] Matter appears differently to our senses due to the nature of its wave-particles. Tolkien seemed to envision this in a symbolic way—the 'Great Music.' Each form of life and matter, and each moment, is a different part of the song.

The most powerful of the Ainur was Melkor, who decided that he was going to make his own song of darkness. Some of the Ainur followed Melkor and the rest stayed in tune with Ilúvatar. The first time Melkor implements his own song, Ilúvatar triumphs over it with his song. The second time, "Melkor rose in uproar and contended with it, and again there was a war of sound more violent than before, until many of the Ainur were dismayed and sang no longer, and Melkor had the mastery."[87] Ilúvatar then rises and triumphs over Melkor's song again. This happens a third time, Ilúvatar still being triumphant. Each of these three uproars has its own theme to how Ilúvatar defeats the counter-song,

---

[86] *Elementary Particles and the Universe* edited by John Schwarz (Cambridge University Press, 2005)
[87] *The Simarillion* by J.R.R. Tolkien, pg. 5 (Ballantine Books., 1982)

marking the Three Ages of Middle-Earth, yet in the metaphysical realm of this Middle-Earth.

Among the Ainur are two classifications: the Maiar and the Valar. The Valar are the higher and the Maiar are lesser. Some of the Maiar were swayed by Melkor and joined the dark side. Among the Maiar that fell to the darkness is Sauron, who is commanded to dwell on Middle-Earth to carry out Melkor's attacks. In a sense, Melkor-Sauron is the demiurge, the physical world in illusion, who is disrupting the creation of the one God and attempting to take his role. On Ilúvatar's side are the higher Ainur, the Valar—the light side—and the rest of the Maiar who stuck to the light side.

Of the Valar there are contrasts of dualities. There are seven female gods and seven male gods. Each of the Valar are archetypes controlling various aspects of life on Middle-Earth. For example, Súlimo is the Lord of the Breath and controls all birds; Ulmo is the Lord of Waters and moves and dwells within all water on Middle-Earth; Varda is the "[...] Lady of the Stars, who knows all the regions of Eä"[88]; Aulë is the Lord of all Substances—"He is a smith and a master of all crafts, and he delights in works of skill, however small, as much as in the mighty buildings of old"[89]; Irmo is the Lord of spiritual visions and dreams; and so forth.

In the beginning of days on Middle-Earth, the Ainur descended and created all life forms, i.e. mosses, grasses, trees, plants, animals, seas, mountains, Humans, Dwarves, Elves, etc. Melkor then counters this, and corrupts some of the men and

---

[88] Ibid, pg. 18
[89] Ibid, pg. 20

elves and turns them into Goblins/Orcs, Wringwraiths, evil Humans, etc., and these become servants of the darkness. Sauron, his chief lieutenant, becomes the Dark Lord in physical manifestation, commanding the 'evil' side at will.

With this cosmology, we have the setting of Middle-Earth. After two 'platonic' ages or cycles have passed and the passing of the third is approaching, we have the background for *The Hobbit* and *The Lord of the Rings* trilogy.

Although there are many distant lands in Middle-Earth, the setting takes place in the 'Western World' and the Western World is thus responsible for the conflict. The story is apropos to a cosmic war between light and darkness, where the one, Sauron, the demiurge of the creation, is aiming to rule over the rest.

The Dark side headed by Sauron is, as a whole, the dragon or monster motif that we find in mythologies from around the world. This 'dragon' is destroying forests for industry and war production, killing living things out of amusement and the desire for power, polluting the environment, and disgracing the sacred. Sauron, who is called the Dark Lord, uses technology to develop ostensibly undefeatable weapons, such as ballistic missiles, in order to take over the world. He is also under the belief that his all-seeing eye is able to watch and know everything.

Here we see the analogies and metaphors that Tolkien uses to fictionally describe the dragon that he saw present in his days. He even hints that he saw this metaphor to be present in our current reality. In a letter he wrote to his son, Christopher, he calls certain dark individuals "lesser servants of Mordor" and orcs.[90]

In perspective, the 'Dark Lord' is epitomizing the Industrial Military Complex and the process of globalization that has been the hegemony of the Western World. The symptoms of this dragon are deforestation, the death of living things for the desire of power, and the pollution of the environment. Ground-breaking technology is immediately converted into an opportunity to improve military capabilities. With the cyber-optic surveillance technologies of the Industrial Military Complex, subsumed with wiretapping, life-accumulated databases, etc., the all-seeing eye is blatantly apparent. Tolkien's ability to enunciate this dragon is only complete when it is slain by the hero.

The hero is likewise as a whole; not one person slays the 'dragon,' but a multitude of individuals. However, there are leaders amongst these individuals. The four Hobbits, Frodo, Sam, Merry, and Pippin exemplify this. With Frodo being the one with the biggest burden and the one who destroys Sauron, it would seem that he is the sole hero. But Frodo would not have gotten far without the aid of the other Hobbits, along with the heroic humans and elves, and the wizard and dwarf whom accompany his endeavors. Thus, the light side is composed of many heroes. Tolkien also soundly establishes that these heroes have an underlying destiny to their lives; for example, Bilbo was meant to find the ring and Frodo was meant to get it from him.

Hobbits are a folk that stick to themselves and are rather oblivious to the world around them. They have never been warlike and do not fight amongst themselves. The law of freewill

---

[90] *The Letters of J.R.R. Tolkien* by J.R.R. Tolkien, pg. 82 (George Allen & Unwin Publishers Ltd., 1981)

is their prevailing governance and they tend to embody a tribal way of council. Coming of age in Hobbit years occurs at the age of thirty-three years old.[91] Thus, Frodo, Sam, Pippin, and Merry have recently come of age after departing on their heroic adventures. In comparison this puts them at the age of a human who is in his or her 20s. It is stressed that the main heroes are young.

Throughout the adventure, the Hobbits are aided by supernatural beings: the elves and the primal man and woman.

The Elves are beings with a very high form of consciousness, knowing and seeing much upon Middle-Earth. Their clandestine way of being keeps their nature concealed from all but those who willfully seek out their counsel. Elves have the ability to communicate with animals, stones and minerals, and plants and trees. The elves do not fear the Dark Lord and his servants, for they dwelled in 'the Blessed Realm.' Tolkien explains that due to this, they live in both the Seen and the Unseen, providing tremendous powers.[92] This implies that the Elves are more deeply rooted in the metaphysical realm—the Blessed Realm— and their presence on Middle-Earth is for protecting the inhabitants on the seen world—they are guardians. The elves live in places where time is seemingly rendered null by their presence, for they are themselves immortal beings (but can still be destroyed). The Elves represent the same motifs that guide the heroes in the mythologies we saw in Part One.

The Hobbits are also helped by Tom Bombadil and his wife Goldberry. Tom Bombadil and Goldberry existed before anything

---

[91] *The Lord of the Rings: The Fellowship of the Ring* by J.R.R. Tolkien, pg. 42 (Ballantine Books)
[92] Ibid, pg. 269

else on Middle-Earth. They are the primal man and woman, 'the Adam and Eve' of Tolkien's world *per se*.

We have here, once again, a very similar resemblance to the mythologies shown in Part One—the guidance of supernatural beings with high intelligence.

Despite this guidance, the world appears to be at an end. Darkness has taken its grasp on the world, killing anything that comes in its way. There is little hope left, as Frodo is carrying the ring to the enemy's doorstep. But Frodo and Sam prevail to destroy the ring of power, casting it in Mount Doom, bringing Sauron's reign to an end. Thus, in climax, with barely any hope left, the light side is triumphant due to the will of two young Hobbits. The dragon/monster archetype has been slain, and life on Middle-Earth experiences a prosperous period of happiness, with a righteous king in reign (Aragorn). This new age is the age of 'Men,' where the mythical beings are no longer in power in the land (i.e. the Elves leave).

Material that Tolkien used in his novels clearly comes right out of the Elder Edda of Scandinavian mythology, on which he lectured at Oxford. More specifically, the story of creation and prophecy of the end of the world, known as the *Völuspá*, or the Sibyl's Prophecy—the more famous poem from the Elder Edda—validates this statement.

In the *Völuspá* are dwarves, giants, dragons, trolls and the names Gandalf, Nori, Kili, Thorin, Fili, Bifur, Bofor, Bombur, Gloin, Dori, and Ori, all names and mythological creatures in Tolkien's tales.

The *Völuspá* is a myth expounding the beginning and end, describing a tribal battle between good and evil, light and dark, cosmos and chaos, life and death. Throughout the tale gods are slain and "[...] the sun turns black, [the] earth sinks in the sea, and fire leaps high about heaven itself."[93] At the beginning of this cosmology, there is nothing. Then the holy ones, the gods, come to raise races of dwarves, Valkyries (Elves), humans, etc. There are three Elven-maidens mighty in wisdom who come from the cosmic tree, which appears to be an elucidation of the three Elven ring-holders at the beginning of Tolkien's Middle-Earth; for, these three of the *Völuspá* made laws, allotted life, and set fate to humans and other life forms.

Then the war between light and dark emerges.

"One in monster's guise was soon to steal the sun from the sky. There feeds he full on the flesh of the dead, And the homes of the gods he reddens with gore; Dark grows the sun, and in summer soon come might storms."[94]

The gods go to council and the dwarfs, 'the masters of stones' roar amongst each other. They then fight against this dark side and end up being triumphant. At the end, an age of righteousness and happiness begins.

Tolkien implemented many other names from ancient Northern cultures into his stories. He writes,

"Frodo is a real name from the Germanic tradition. Its Old English form was *Fróda*. Its obvious [connection] is with the old word *fród* meaning etymologically 'wise by experience,' but it had mythological [connections] with legends of the

---

93 *Essential Sacred Writing From Around the World* by Mircea Eliade, pg. 119 (Harper & Row, 1992)
94 Ibid, pgs. 123-4

Golden Age in the North."[95]

In a different letter he explains that many of the other names come from what he calls "the Ancient and Elvish World (of Northern mythology) (parenthesis are mine).[96]

In the first of Tolkien's Middle-Earth novels, *The Hobbit*, Tolkien uses 'goblins' to describe what become Orcs in *The Lord of the Rings*. Goblins are an archetype in mythologies from around the world—found in Japan,[97] Ireland,[98] Korea,[99] India,[100] Germany,[101] Incan mythology,[102] African mythology[103] and other mythologies.

"Some very rare 'goblin' runes in the service of vengeance, sorceries, and other magic signs are to be found on Rökstenen near Omberg, Sweden, one of the most

---

[95] *The Letters of J.R.R. Tolkien* by J.R.R. Tolkien, pg. 224 (George Allen & Unwin Publishers Ltd., 1981)

[96] Ibid, pg. 31

[97] *Civilization and Monsters* by Gerald Figal, pg. 83 (Duke University Press, 1999)

[98] *An Etymological Dictionary of the English Language*, by Walter William Skeat, pg. 475 (Clarendon Press, 1898)

[99] *Han'guk chŏnt'ong sasang* by Won Park, pg. 110 (Inha University Press, 2002)

[100] *The Presence of Śiva* by Stella Kramrisch, pg. 395 (Princeton University Press, 1992)

[101] *Teutonic mythology, Volume 4* by Jacob Grimm, pg. 1433 (W. Swan Sonnenschein & Allen, 1888)

[102] *From Viracocha to the Virgin of Copacabana* by Verónica Reese, pg.107 (University of Texas Press, 1997)

[103] *Introductory Sketch of the Bantu Language* by Alice Werner, pg. 46 (E. P. Dutton & CO., 1919)

wonderful memorials from the Viking Age in Scandinavia."[104]

The mythological goblin is always summarized as either a supernatural being that is dark, grotesque, and monster-like or a human that is dark and evil.

As mentioned above, the goblins and orcs are under the control of Sauron, and ultimately Melkor's command. Sauron wants to control Middle-Earth for his own, and uses his armies of orcs to kill off what is good in this world. We find similar motifs among the deities of destruction in Vedic philosophy. Maheśvara is an epithet of Śiva the destroyer, in Hinduism.

> "Maheśvara, the Great Lord, replied to the Goddess that in the past he had been looking a long time for a pure place to dwell in. He could not find one, was frustrated, and out of anger against procreation he created the terrible piśācas, flesh-eating ghouls and goblins, and the rākṣasas, intent on killing people."[105]

Besides goblins, Tolkien uses other mythical beings. We have already seen dragons persistent in the mythologies from around the world, which Tolkien uses in *The Hobbit* and *The Lord of the Rings*. Then there are the stone giants which fight amongst each other. Giants show up in Semitic,[106] Hindu,[107] Native American,[108]

---

[104] *Scandinavian Review, Volume 9* by American-Scandinavian Foundation, pg. 320 (American-Scandinavian Foundation, 1921)

[105] *The Presence of Śiva* by Stella Kramrisch, pg. 395 (Princeton University Press, 1992)

[106] *The Jewish study Bible*, pg. 21 (Oxford University Press, 2004)

[107] *The origins of evil in Hindu mythology* by Wendy O'Flaherty, pg. 69 (University of California Press, 1980)

South American,[109] Greek, Norse,[110] Slavic,[111] and Chinese[112] mythologies.

Tolkien's mythical world Middle-Earth embodies archetypes that we find in the global esoteric traditions. In Middle-Earth, mountains are held as sacred places where secrets that have survived the ages are still shrouded within. "Everything in [the Forest] is very much alive, more aware of what is going on, so to speak, than things are in the Shire."[113] Furthermore animals are conscious entities with their own form of communication and intelligence.

For the Bön, Hindus, Buddhists, and Jains, specific mountains are the homes to certain deities, sources of powers and gateways to the cosmic axis.[114] This is a pattern that shows up in all mythologies; Mircea Eliade writes:

"Mountains are the nearest thing to the sky, and are thence endowed with a twofold holiness: on one hand they share in the spatial symbolism of transcendence—they are 'high,'

---

[108] *American Anthropologist, Volume 2*, pg. 7 (American Anthropological Association, 1889)

[109] *Inca myths* by Gary Urton, pg. 21 (University of Texas, 1999)

[110] *Norse Mythology* by John Lindow, pg. 2 (Oxford University Press, 2002)

[111] *Folklore of Other Lands* by Selvi, Kahn, and Soule, pg. 167 (S. F. Vanni, 1956)

[112] *Chinese myths* by Anne Birrell, pg. 28 (University of Texas Press, 2000)

[113] *The Lord of the Rings: The Fellowship of the Ring* by J.R.R. Tolkien, pg. 144 (Ballantine Books)

[114] *Bө & Bön* by Dmitry Ermakov, pg. 11-2 (Vajra Publications, 2010)

'vertical', 'supreme,' and so on—and on the other, they are the especial domain of all hierophanies of atmosphere, and therefore, the dwelling of the gods. Every mythology has its sacred mountain, some more or less famous variation on the Greek Olympus. All sky gods have a certain high place set apart for their worship. The symbolic and religious significance of mountains is endless. Mountains are often looked on as the place where sky and earth meet, a "central point" therefore, the point through which the Axis Mundi goes, a region impregnated with the sacred, a spot where one can pass from one cosmic zone to another."[115]

Likewise, forests are held to be the dwelling place of gods and goddesses in mythologies.[116] The trees of the forest hold the same nature as the mountains, in that they symbolize the cosmic axis.

The "world-mythological" view on animals is also in par with Tolkien's. David Leeming writes, "Animals in mythologies typically belong to an age when humans and animals could communicate directly."[117] Many ancient civilizations depicted deities (archetypes) as either partially or entirely animal.

On a further note, magic occurs in the Middle-Earth due to sound vibrations, via song or vocal incantations. This is seen when Tom Bombadil sings Merry free from a tree that has him captive and then heals him with a song incantation; or when the spoken words of the Elven-tongue put an enchanting spell on its

---

[115] *Patterns in Comparative Religion* by Mircea Eliade, pgs. 99-100 (University of Nebraska Press, 1996)
[116] Ibid, pg. 272
[117] *Oxford Companion to World Mythology* by David Leeming, pg. 18 (Oxford University Press, 2005)

listeners. The vibrations of their words take shape with the ability to induce visions in the listener. Gandalf casts spells using incantations that have affects such as locking and unlocking doors.

The inscription of symbols for magical purposes also plays its role in 'the Tolkien Tales.' Tolkien uses the Scandinavian hieroglyphs, runes, in his stories to do so. His runes have the ability to ward off perils and wounds when written on shields, to encourage triumphant victories in battles when carved on swords and other weapons, and so forth. Tolkien's use of runes reminds us of the actual use of runes in Scandinavian and Mongolian lore, that was illustrated in *Volume 1*

5 THE ALCHEMICAL SEVEN

"In the language of initiations, 'seven' stands for the highest stage of illumination and would therefore be the coveted goal of all desire." – Carl Jung[118]

It is summer in the year 1990 and a train is en route to London from Manchester. A delay has caused the train to sit still, and the passengers who are attentive are looking out at the majestic valleys of green, woven with sinuously blue rivers, besmirched by the industrial activities of super chimpanzees. In a flashing strike of lightning, an idea is painted in the mind of a mother on welfare, struggling to make ends meet. She thinks: "Did this idea really just fall into my head?"[119] Magical! She had been studying the classics for a while—from Greek mythology to Renaissance alchemy—and made a keen study of the master story-teller J.R.R. Tolkien, so her conscious was finally ripe enough

---

[118] *Dreams* by C.G. Jung, pg. 137 (Princeton University Press, 1974)

[119] J.K. Rowling in an interview with Scholastic (February, 2000)

for *the unconscious* to flow into vision.[120]

Seven is a powerful number, a complete number. So a glimpse of seven years has been seen. Frantically searching for something to write the vision down on, she finds a napkin. This will do—for she can't miss this—this will become her apogee. This is her answer. The archetype has revealed what will grip the masses with an esoteric code hidden within.

In her vision she saw how to write a story appealing to both genders that grew with the reader. This would allow the interest to last in order for her to write 4,224 pages in seventeen years. Knowing that a large number of children and teenagers would ultimately read the series—whose reality tunnels have not yet been entirely molded by society and the status quo—she embedded esoteric and occult ideas and historical individuals into the series. This act subliminally caused the reader to store this information in the subconscious. With a fictionalized plotline that sparks the imagination, Rowling found an archetypal creation to bestow historical information unknown to the masses while hiding analogies and metaphors relevant to the society of today.

Where Tolkien's tale ends with the age of Men, Rowling's tale begins. The conflict of the story is once again a product of the Western World. The heroic adventure is about humans who have the capability of performing magic. Most of the world's population are Muggles, who can't perform magic because they don't 'see' and 'hear' properly.[121] Muggles generally watch TV

---

[120] Note: This vision on a train is rather similar to Albert Einstein's vision on a street car, where he conceptualized special relativity.
[121] *Harry Potter and the Prisoner of Azkaban* by J.K. Rowling, pg. 36 (Scholastic, 1999)

most of the time and are ignorant. The witches and wizards are the focus of the story, however, and these humans involved are a contrast between duality: dark and light.

The Dark Lord (Lord Voldemort) and his regime is the dragon archetype whose imperialism aims to control the world. He wants to kill off all of the Muggles to create a world of only 'pureblood' lineages. He kills for fun and power, and controls the lives of everyone around him. He has various sorts of followers and entities on his side, just as Sauron. When he comes back to full power he controls the media and the magical government to try to enable global genocide. The magical government then uses a 'top-wanted' scapegoat (analogous to the terrorist scapegoat of today) to try to bring down all of the resistance, and as there are many people looking for the main members of the resistance, this represents the same sort of 'All-Seeing Eye.'

The Dark Lord character symbolizes the demiurge archetype; however, in this new age of men, the demiurge comes and goes in human embodiment. Rowling writes, "The Dark Arts are many, varied, ever-changing, and eternal. Fighting them is like fighting a many-headed monster, which, each time a neck is severed, sprouts a head even fiercer and cleverer than before."[122] Grindelwald was the last 'Dark Lord' who was defeated by Albus Dumbeldore. The old hero, Dumbeldore, then becomes the 'guide' of the new hero, Harry Potter.

The 'light side' has many heroes involved in the 'slaying of the dragon' but is centered around Harry Potter and his 'best' friends Ron Weasley and Hermione Granger. The story shows their lives

---

[122] Harry Potter and the Half-Blood Prince by J.K. Rowling, pg. 177 (Scholastic, 2005)

from the ages of ten to seventeen, or their coming of age in Rowling's story. The demiurge failed to destroy Harry Potter at the age of one; and, in effect, their destinies have become intertwined. Harry's parents die saving Harry, which activates the very ancient and powerful form of magic, love. The Dark Lord is forced into hiding, and each book shows a year of his rise back to power and the heroic adventures combating this rise. The *ancient* magic acts as a supernatural guide that protects Harry until he ultimately destroys the Dark Lord at the end of the story.

The archetypes within Tolkien's tale are still apparent, but they have taken a new form—a new image. The wise old man that Gandalf represents is manifest in the wizard Albus Dumbeldore. The young hobbit heroes who 'slay the dragon' are now adolescent wizards and witches; the main protagonist, Frodo, is in comparison with Harry Potter. Instead of the supernatural guide archetypes being Elves and the primal man and woman that we see in Tolkien's tale, they take the form of dead spirits and powerful *ancient* magic. Harry's dead parents' spirits, James and Lily Potter, in a certain sense, represent the primal man and woman. Further, other dead spirits give supernatural guidance in various moments. Like the Hobbits, these young heroes also receive aid from many other individuals who have a wide range of personalities.

The demiurge archetypes, Sauron and Voldemort, have similar followers. The Wringwraiths and Dementors represent the same sort of deathly, dark and powerful spirits that are servants to each 'Dark Lord.' The Orc leaders and the Death Eaters are in comparison; each command 'armies.' Each Dark Lord is extremely powerful and in the climaxes of both stories, their power almost has its clench on the entire world—there is little hope left. But the heroes prevail and defeat the demiurge.

Then there are the mythological archetypes that Rowling implements. Rowling uses basilisks, centaurs, griffins, phoenixes, sphinxes, veelas (*Vilas*), ghouls, ghosts, dwarfs, merpeople, leprechauns, werewolves, goblins, unicorns, dragons, giants, and gnomes in her stories—all creatures we find in mythologies from around the world, many of which Tolkien uses as well.

As Tolkien structured his tale off of Northern European mythology, Rowling structures hers on Hermetic mythology.

The first book, entitled *Harry Potter and the Philosopher's Stone* or the Americanized title *Harry Potter and the Sorcerer's Stone,* demonstrates the alchemical foundation of the entire seven. The physical Philosopher's Stone (the symbol of the process of transmuting the consciousness into a golden state) is being protected at the Hogwarts School of Witchcraft and Wizardry because the Dark Lord is seeking it, in order to come back into body. Rowling writes,

> "The ancient study of alchemy is concerned with making the [Philosopher's] Stone, a legendary substance with astonishing powers. The stone will transform any metal into pure gold. It also produces the Elixir of Life, which makes the drinker immortal. There have been many reports of the [Philosopher's] Stone over the centuries, but the only Stone currently in existence belongs to Mr. Flamel, who celebrated his six hundred and sixty-fifth birthday last year [and] enjoys a quiet life in Devon with his wife, Parenelle (six hundred and

fifty-eight)."[123]

Nicholas Flamel was an intellectual, a manuscript dealer and an alchemist born in 1330, in Paris, France. A man with a mysterious book that had a copper cover and pages made of tree rinds scripted with hieroglyphs came into contact with Flamel; Flamel then purchased this book for only 2 florins. Flamel states that the book had *three* times *seven* pages in total.[124] This book was authored by Abraham the Jew, who is also the alleged co-author of an esoteric treatise called *Abramelin the Mage*, published in several manuscripts in Germany during the Rosicrucian Renaissance.

Flamel portrays the man whom he bought the book from as a veritably wise man who was patiently waiting through time for the moment when 'the Messiahs' will come and destroy 'the kings' and return the righteous reign to Earth. The book then set Flamel on an esoteric quest.

In *Exposition of the Hieroglyphical Figures*, Flamel describes this mysterious book and how it ultimately led him to his discovery of the Philosopher's Stone. The descriptions of the hieroglyphs in the book are a caduceus; a crucified serpent; a wilderness scene; symbols for the process of transmuting metals; enlightened figures; Hermes holding the caduceus wand; the god Mercury; an old man with an hourglass crown and a scythe symbolizing time and death; a four-leafed flower on top of the cosmic Mountain surrounded by 'the Dragons and Griffons of the North'; a garden with the cosmic tree and fountain; and the

---

[123] *Harry Potter and the Sorcerer's Stone* by J.K. Rowling, pg. 220 (Scholastic, 1998)
[124] *The Jewish alchemists* by Raphael Patai, pg. 219 (Princeton University Press, 1994)

demiurge archetype, King Herod, killing innocent children. The mantras activated cycling levels of awareness in Flamel, as he explains that he studied and contemplated the hieroglyphs night and day, and then the alchemical transmutation began to occur within his consciousness.

On Isaac Newton and Gottfried Leibniz's quests to discover the Philosopher's Stone, they read the famous 17th century alchemist Eirenaeus Philalethes. Philalethes writes that if one wants to understand the Philosopher's Stone and discover the Elixir of Life:

"[They should] learn to know, who the Companions of *Cadmus* are, and what that *Serpent* is which devoured them, what the hollow *Oak* is which *Cadmus* fastened the *Serpent* through and through unto; Learn what *Diana's Doves* are, which do vanquish the *Lion* by asswaging him; I say the Green *Lion*, which is in very deed the *Babylonian Dragon*, killing all things with his Poyson: Then at length learn to know the *Caducean Rod* of *Mercury*, with which he worketh Wonders, and what the *Nymphs* are, which he [calls] by Incantation, if thou desirest to enjoy thy wish."[125]

We can see the pattern that shows up between Philalethes' and Flamel's explanations. The symbolism portrays a person who has transformed his or her consciousness and has vanquished the imperialist archetype, being guided by higher forms of consciousness along the way. It has the same features of the heroic stories we saw in Part One.

After much study and epiphany, Flamel's reading of the book leads him to discover the Philosopher's Stone. With the ability to

---

[125] *Secrets Reveal'd* by Eirenaeus Philalethes, pg. 6

make gold, Flamel gives his riches to charities and he builds several hostels and churches. In the churches he painted alchemical hieroglyphs to guide others on their paths.

Some academic sources state that Flamel died in 1418, at the age of 88, because there is ample evidence in his will that he built his own tombstone for 'when it was needed.'[126] However, Flamel dedicated much time into creating two bas-reliefs on his tombstone that shows a different perspective. On his tombstone there are two parts: on the bottom bas-relief Flamel's ego is portrayed dead and in the bas-relief above is the heroic archetype (in the image of Jesus Christ) achieving immortality. He is surrounded by other supernatural beings and is being handed a book and a key from St. Peter and a book and a sword from St. Paul. The Sun and the Moon flame and shine on the sides of the hero's head—a symbol for unifying duality.[127]

Other academic sources reveal a different story than Flamel's death at the age of 88. Paul Lucas was a merchant and naturalist who lived from 1664-1737. He traveled throughout the Mediterranean, going to places such as Greece and Egypt. When traveling in Asia Minor, in 1714, Lucas met a Tartar from Uzbekistan who looked peculiar. The man told Lucas that he was one of seven men who travel the world seeking wisdom.

> "[He] hinted he was in possession of the philosopher's stone, which would prolong the life of the philosopher to an antediluvian period. Paul Lucas smiled incredulously.—Nicholas Flamel and Perenelle possessed the secret, but they died (as we all must die) three hundred years ago.—Great

---

[126] *Metamorphosis of a Death Symbol* by Kathleen Cohen, pgs. 90-103 (University of California Press, 1973)
[127] Ibid.

was his surprise, when, in answer to this observation, the [man] stated that Nicholas Flamel and Perenelle were yet living; he had seen them in India about three years before, and they were his dearest friends."[128]

This sighting is nearly three centuries after Flamel's supposed death. The answer to the anomaly is a question: to live the myth or not?

Immortality shows up in mythologies on every continent on Earth. In China,

> "The magician Li Chao Kuin advises the Emporor Wu Ti of the Han dynasty as follows: 'Sacrifice to the furnace (*tsao*) and you will be able to summon (supernatural) beings; when you have called forth these beings, the powder of cinnabar can be transformed into yellow gold; when the yellow gold is produced you will be able to make of it utensils for drinking and eating and in so doing you will have a prolonged longevity. When your longevity is prolong you will be able to see the blessed [beings] (*hsien*) of the island of P'eng Lai which is in the midst of the seas. When you have seen them and have made the *feng* and *chan* sacrifices [of food and jade ritual items], then you will not die.'"[129]

In the Brahmanic texts of India, the initiate—also through archetypal sacrifices—achieves immortality and joins the gods.

---

[128] *The Collected Historical Works of Sir Francis Palgrave, K.H.*, pgs. 310-1 (Cambridge University Press Archive)
[129] *The Forge and the Crucible: The Origins and Structures of Alchemy* by Mircea Eliade, pg. 112 (University of Chicago Press, 1978)

"Whoever knows the mystery of that initiation has triumphed over the second death (*punarmrtyu*) and fears death no longer."[130] The immortality quest shows up with Osiris in ancient Egypt and Gilgamesh in Babylon,[131] in South East Asian mythology,[132] Incan mythology[133], Aztec mythology,[134] and many other mythologies. Mircea Eliade writes about this pattern,

> "The combat with the monster seems, from all one can see, to have had the quality of an initiation; [one] must 'prove [oneself]', become a 'hero', to have the right to possess immortality. Anyone who cannot defeat the dragon or the serpent can have no access to the Tree of Life, can never attain immortality."

It is evident that this phenomenon is an archetype within mythic reality.

On top of the Philosopher's Stone (the immortality symbol) being the basis of Rowling's first book, she incorporated further Hermetic ideas of the Rosicrucians into the plotlines of all seven books. The secret society of Renaissance Europe, the Fraternitas Rosæ Crucis, combated the imperialistic 'dragon' of the Hapsburg House and the Catholic Church present in its society. This Rosicrucian movement of medieval Europe used the symbol of Christian Rosenkreutz as its leader or model. Christian

---

[130] *Patterns in Comparative Religion* by Mircea Eliade, pg. 96 (University of Nebraska Press, 1996)
[131] Ibid, pg. 140
[132] *Asian Mythologies* edited by Yves Bonnefoy, pg. 229 (University of Chicago Press, 1993)
[133] *Religion in the Andes* by Sabine MacCormack, pg. 90 (Princeton University Press, 1991)
[134] *Handbook to Life in the Aztec World* by Manuel Moreno, pg. 164 (Oxford University Press, 2007)

Rosenkreutz was a wise old man who lived to be 106 years old. His symbol of the secret society manifests in Rowling's work in a two-fold manner.

The former hero, Albus Dumbeldore, represents the older Christian Rosenkreutz—Albus Dumbeldore lived to be 116 years old. He is the leader of the secret society, the Order of the Phoenix, which combats the imperialism of the Dark Lord.

On another level, the younger Christian Rosenkreutz mimics the heroic journeys of Harry Potter. First note that Harry Potter also is the leader of a secret society that combats the Dark Lord, Dumbeldore's Army. *The Chymical Wedding of Christian Rosenkreutz* is the third original manuscript of the Fraternitas Rosæ Crucis published in 1450. This story tells of Christian Rosenkreutz going through seven days or 'journeys' that he must succeed in for transformation.

Rosenkreutz is delivered a letter from an angel (*Faërie*) that asks him to join an alchemical wedding on the cosmic mountain. His first 'journey' is to prove his courage and go to a castle and pursue the secrets of nature. He chooses to do so and goes to a castle where 'miracles' happen; there are moving portraits, and the castle is near a body of water where nymphs live. Rosenkreutz has to choose between four paths: a difficult path, an easy path, a fun path, and a incorruptible path; he chose the difficult path.

In the next journey, Rosenkreutz "[...] gives up bread, uses [the] qualities of balance, [and] the compass,"[135] which are symbols for his being finding direction and beginning to learn how to balance out the dualities of life.

In the third journey he has to give up water—a symbol for sacrificing one's emotions.

For the fourth journey, Rosenkreutz gives up salt. The salt the Rosicrucians are referring to is the alchemical one, which symbolizes the substance, or the body of something.

For the fifth journey he gives up his outer garments to reveal his naked self. This symbolizes giving up all personalities and ideals (outer garments) that distract him from his essence (naked body).

In the sixth, he demonstrates his humility by staying behind, which brings a crisis and he faces opposition.

In the seventh he must prove himself in the front of the scales at a weighting ceremony.

---

[135] *The Chemical Wedding of Christian Rosenkreutz* edited by Joscelyn Godwin, pg.114 (Weiser, 1991)

The symbolism of these journeys aligns to the themes of Harry Potter's seven years, or journeys.

In his first year, Harry receives a letter inviting him to a castle where magic happens, portraits move, and there is a lake where merpeople (nymphs) live (along with the other mythical creatures living in Rowling's magical world). Harry then proves his courage by stopping the Dark Lord from getting the Philosopher's Stone.

In his second year, Harry goes to the Chamber of Secrets and has to prove that he is a true Gryffindor by triumphing over the Dark Lord again. This shows that he has found direction and is beginning to learn to balance out dualities.

In the third year, Harry has to get rid of his hate-filled emotions toward Sirius Black whom he believed help kill his parents. Otherwise he would kill his innocent godfather and let the true servant of the Dark Lord live (Peter Pettigrew). He triumphs again.

The result of the fourth year is the return of the Dark Lord into body, which occurs from a sacrifice of Harry's blood, or substance.

Harry's fifth year is one filled with resentment. Harry is left out of the loop of what is going on with Voldemort from individuals he regards as 'parent-like' figures, while Voldemort wants to kill him (i.e. Dumbeldore won't even look at him). He is pestered by the magical government and the media throughout the year, and he is made fun of by many of his peers. However, this process strips these 'outer garments' down to his 'essence' and he proceeds to pursue what he is destined to do.

The climax of the sixth year is a crisis; the Dark Lord (the opposition) takes control of the world and kills Harry's guide, Dumbledore. With this crisis Harry must now 'stay behind' and refrain from attending Hogwarts for his final year, in order to destroy the Dark Lord. This demonstrates his humility, for he is willing to sacrifice his life to the cause.

The seventh year is the weighting ceremony. Harry's determination is weighted and he passes by sacrificing his life to destroy the Dark Lord. However, this sacrifice brings a resurrection to his being. He ultimately survives and unifies what was duality.

Rowling also uses other motifs from this 15th century manifesto. Rosenkreutz is pestered by violent dreams; for example he dreams of a door that he cannot open and he sees 'Royals' being carried away by Death. Harry Potter has a recurring dream in his fifth year where he is trying to get through a passageway and he also foresees the attempted-murder of Arthur Weasley, which saves Arthur's life. There is "[...] a skull or death's head with a serpent eternally circling through the eye holes,"[136] which is the 'Death Mark' symbol in Harry Potter. There is a phoenix that attacks a serpent, dies and is reborn in fire (year two of Harry Potter).

Besides the embodiment of the transformation symbolism from this manifesto, Rowling uses further elements from the Rosicrucian movement.

In Flamel and Philalethes' descriptions of alchemical transformation, the hero expands his or her consciousness, is guided by supernatural beings, there is a battle between a griffin and a dragon (the imperialism archetype), and the hero

---

[136] Ibid, pg. 131

understands the nature of the demiurge (in the symbol of King Herod/Babylonian Dragon).

The hippogriff, or griffin, is an anthropomorphic creature that has eagle wings, an eagle head, and a lion's body. This creature shows up in Ariosto's literature from Medieval Italy, and it transports individuals from place to place.[137] This same motif is found in Persian, Babylonian, Assyrian, Akkadian, Greek, Chinese, and Hindu mythology—always being a winged 'beast' that guards the sanctuary, a symbol of divine power.[138] The diversity of this archaic symbol proves it is archetypal.

Rowling uses the hippogriff not only as a magical creature that transports people from place to place, but also as the mascot of the Griffindor House and the House of the hero. The Griffindor House is the one that ultimately protects Hogwarts, or the sanctuary. The Griffindor House is brave and is symbolized by the lion.

The Dragon takes its form in the Slytherin House—the Dark Lord is the heir to Slytherin and many of his supporters come from that house. The Dark Lord's regime is the 'King Herod' archetype. Slytherin is the House of power and its symbol is the serpent.

These two make up the first pair of the alchemical *quaternio* of Hermetic thought. The classical element of Fire within the microcosm is passion, creativity; Water is emotions—power. The classical element Air represents intelligence; and Earth represents

---

[137] *The Cambridge History of Italian Literature* edited by Peter brand and Lino Pertile, pg. 237 (Cambridge University Press, 1999)
[138] *Angels* by David Jones, pgs. 14-5 (Oxford University Press, 2011)

hard-work and patience.

The other two Houses in Harry Potter, Ravenclaw and Huffelpuff, align to these latter classical elements. Ravenclaw's symbol is the eagle and its students are witty and intelligent—Air. Huffelpuff's symbol is the badger, an animal that burrows itself in the Earth and its students are hard-workers—Earth.

Then there are the main subjects that the students are taught at Hogwarts: Astronomy, Divination, History of Magic, Defense Against the Dark Arts, Charms, Transfiguration, Potions, and Herbology.

In Herboloy, students learn about different magical plants and what their effects are. Paracelsus is a character in Rowling's story. Paracelsus is also a historical alchemist who spent much time to discover the effects of plants in many different lands. With success, Paracelsus found healing powers in certain plants and cured many people's ailments with alchemical extracts.[139] Herbology mimics an aspect of Paracelsian alchemy.

Potions class is the other aspect, as students mix plants and other ingredients in a cauldron, and use water, fire, earth, and air to create potions. This aspect of Paracelsian alchemy was practiced by the Medieval European alchemists, but is also found throughout other mythologies. Mircea Eliade writes about its trace in ancient cultures.

"There is magic power in water; cauldrons, kettles, chalices, are all receptacles of this magic force which is often symbolized by some divine liquor such as ambrosia or 'living

---

[139] *Paracelsus* by Andrew Weeks, pg. 28 (State University of New York Press, 1997)

water'; they confer immortality or eternal youth, or they change whoever owns them into a hero or a god, etc."[140]

In Defense Against the Dark Arks, Charms, and Transfiguration class, students use magic wands and invocations to cast spells. Invocations were also the way magic was carried out in the Lord of the Rings (along with the wizard's staff).

The etymology of the incantations that Rowling uses comes mostly from the Latin language, but is also derived from other archaic languages. In an open-interview on April 15th, 2004, Rowling asked the audience: "Does anyone know *where avada kedavra* came from? It is an ancient spell in Aramaic, and it is the original of abracadabra, which means 'let the thing be destroyed.'" In Latin, *accio* means to call forth, or to summon. In Harry Potter, *accio* is the spell that is used to summon an object to the witch or wizard casting the spell; cave means 'to beware' and *inimicum* means to 'the enemy.' Rowling uses the phrase *cave inimicum* as a spell to protect an area from enemies. *Crucio* means to torture in Latin, which corresponds to the torture spell in Harry Potter. The majority of the other incantations follow this Latin etymology.

In Latin Europe, "Pronouncing magic words is one of the chief activities of wizards (*magi* in Latin), who practice the art of magic or *ars magica*.[141] In Rosicrucianism, we find the use of wands and the pronunciation of Latin incantations (as well as incantations in other archaic languages) to perform magic. "When the Magician flourishes the Wand it is to be conceived that [one] takes upon

---

[140] *Patterns in Comparative Religion* by Mircea Eliade, pg. 207 (University of Nebraska Press, 1996)
[141] *A Natural History of Latin* by Tore Janson, pg. 161 (Oxford University Press, 2007)

[oneself] the authority and wisdom of Tahuti (or Thoth, the god of Heka, or magic) before the council of the cosmic Gods (or archetypes)" (parenthesis are mine).[142] The idea is to use the wand as a way to amplify the energy that one is emitting through the thought process and the vibrations coming from the word(s) being pronounced, in order for the observer (the magician) to change what he or she is observing.

Carl Jung reported that he had the pleasure of meeting 'rustic' wizards who used Merseburg magic spell incantations in High German to produce extraordinary effects; such as curing any ailment and filling enclosed areas (i.e. houses) with spirits.[143]

The Bön shamans of Central Asia had the magical capabilities of causing flowers to rain, to heal serious ailments, fly in the sky, become animals, repel black magic, overcome enemies, transform themselves into animals, destroy black magicians, make rivers flow upstream, 'stupefy' people making them fall to the ground, curse people, and bring peace.[144] Similar magical powers are found with the shamans of South and North America, Europe, Australia, and Africa.[145]

In her third book, Rowling mentions how fascinating the ancient Egyptian magicians were and how some of their curses and spells still exist today. In ancient Egypt, we find remnants of

---

[142] *The Tree of Life* by Israel Regardie, pg. 163 (Llewellyn Publications, 2001)
[143] *Flying Saucers* by Carl Jung, pg. 64 (Princeton University Press, 1978)
[144] *Bө & Bön* by Dmitry Ermakov, pgs. 583-687 (Vajra Publications, 2010)
[145] *Magic: A Sociological Study* by Hutton Webster (Stanford University Press Archive)

magic that show transfiguration spells to transform the deceased, spells to protect against serpents, to turn an individual into an animal, to heal ailments, invoke archetypal energies, and so forth.[146] "Magical spells were typically to be recited to or over an image in order to be effective. The magic of images and the magic of words complemented one another in their effectiveness, so as to visualize the sacred."[147]

These magical capabilities show up throughout the ancient world. In ancient China, there are spells that permit one to flee.[148]

> "In the ancient Greco-Roman world, it was common practice to curse or bind an enemy or rival by writing an incantation on a tablet and dedicating it to a god or spirit. These curses or binding spells, commonly called defixiones were intended to bring other people under power and control those who commissioned them. More than a thousand such texts, written between the 5th Century B.C.E. and the 5th Century C.E., have been discovered from North Africa to England, and from Syria to Spain."[149]

The *imperius* (Latin for: to command) curse in Harry Potter mimics these curses, as it allows its caster to completely command the person it hits, at his or her pleasing.

---

[146] *The Cannibal Hymn* by Christopher Eyre pg. 62 (Liverpool University Press, 2002)

[147] *Death and Salvation in Ancient Egypt* by Jan Assmann, pg. 240 (Cornell University Press, 2005)

[148] *China under Jurchen rule: essays on Chin intellectual and cultural history* edited by Hoyt Tillman and Stephen Vest, pg. 247 (State University of New York Press, 1995)

[149] *Curse Tablets and Binding Spells from the Ancient World* by John Gager, back cover (Oxford University Press, 1992)

The magic wand is also an archetype that we find in mythologies. Hermes held a golden wand that could put people to sleep, awaken people, rouse and lead spirits, and so forth.[150] We find magical wands with the early Christians,[151] the ancient Egyptians,[152] in Norse mythology,[153] in Mesoamerican mythology,[154] and in many other mythologies.

In South East Asian mythology there is a story of a poor and husbandless mother who supernaturally gets impregnated. She is guided by 'supernatural' tigers who bring her food until she gives birth to a boy who becomes a woodcutter.

> "Then, one day, he received a magic wand from the hands of a god; this instrument enabled him to resuscitate the dead or kill people, depending on which end he pointed at the subject in question. In addition, this divinity charged him with guarding the mountain Tan-Vien. After this boy brought many dead people back to life. He became a doctor as well, tending to the diseases of simple people whom he sought out himself. The people expressed their admiration for him and gave him

[150] *Essential Sacred Writing From Around the World* by Mircea Eliade, pg. 372(Harper & Row, 1992)
[151] *Ancient Christian Magic: Coptic Texts of Ritual Power* edited by Marvin Richard, pg. 325 (Princeton University Press, 1999)
[152] Religion and Ritual in Ancient Egypt by Emily Teer, pg. 169 (Cambridge University Press, 2011)
[153] *Norse Mythology* by Rasmus Anderson pg. 357 (S.C. Griggs, 1884)
[154] *Latin American Indian Literatures, Volume 1-3* by the Department of Hispanic Languages and Literatures (University of Pittsburgh Press, 1977)

the title of god of the mountain."[155]

Divination and Astronomy class go hand-in-hand, as Rowling explains the true form of Divination taught by the supernatural centaur, Firenze. This form of divination occurs by observing the stars overhead to find out about the future. It may take several years to even begin to see that something is going to happen. This form of divination is not definite—no prediction is definite. The centaur also uses herbal incenses to divine.

On the other hand, Rowling states that human divination is an imprecise form of magic. However, one can enter into a non-physical world via the "Inner Eye," or the pineal gland, to learn things about the past and future.[156] One has to first broaden their mind and "[...] allow [one's] eyes to see past the mundane," entering into the world of patterns. By contemplating patterns one can receive information on past or future events. A form of tarot cards, dream interpretation, and tea reading are methods for deciphering these patterns.

---

[155] *Asian Mythologies* edited by Yves Bonnefoy, pg. 229 (University of Chicago Press, 1993)
[156] *Harry Potter and the Prisoner of Azkaban* by J.K. Rowling, pgs. 102-3 (Scholastic, 1999)

6 SPARKING A NEURAL SYNAPSE

"Mythical drama reminded men that suffering is never final; that death is always followed by resurrection; that every defeat is annulled and transcended by the final victory."
Mircea Eliade[157]

With *The Lord of the Rings/The Hobbit* series and the *Harry Potter* series being among the two best-selling book series in history, we must look into what this implies psychologically. There is no doubt that both Tolkien and Rowling are great writers, but there is something else that triggered each series' ability to grip the masses—their archetypal nature. Overall, each tale shows a story of a young hero who defeats the imperialism archetype, bringing a period of peace to 'Earth.' In Part One, we saw that this was the same plotline of the heroic stories we found in the mythologies on every single continent. As these mythologies have been told as long as written history, this heroic ordeal is engrained into our psyche. It is also hinted that this heroic ordeal is even older than humanity, as we find it at the beginning of

---

[157] *Cosmos and History* by Mircea Eliade, pg. 101 (Harper Touchbooks, 1959)

written history and it has been manifesting itself in the ages and cultures since. It appears as an archetype.

Its relentless presence poses to those who are cognitive of its existence: are you ready to live the myth yet?

By looking into the myth in more detail we see that the end of the path to the *complete* embodiment of 'hero' is not instantaneous—the myths of Tolkien, Rowling, and the 'dragon-slayers' from various cultures are truly describing the last part of this path to the great salvation. This will be shown by examining the following mythologies related to this concept.

The Bhagavad Gita is one of the many ancient scriptures from India.[158] Its setting begins with a young prince, Arjuna, whose kingdom loses its control to a new imperialistic King. The resistance expects Arjuna to become the leader and take back the Kingdom.

The story starts with Krishna (a hero-archetype of India) counseling Arjuna. Arjuna explains that he doesn't want to fight—he believes killing is evil—and throws down his weapons. Krishna then explains to Arjuna the nature of death, that the physical body is what experiences death, but the soul is immortal. The soul cycles through physical bodies in the attempt to remove itself from all karma until it has unified duality and achieved the glory of the gods. The soul must combat the evil in the world (the 'dragon') that it is bound to, in order to become its true essence. Krishna encourages that through selfless service (to the cause), renunciation (out of the outer garments of life), and meditation (inner-contemplation), one is choosing to take a path to fight the

---

[158] *The Bhagavad Gita* translated by Winthrop Sargeant (State University of New York Press, 2009)

evil side. The great choice, though, as Krishna puts it, lies within the self to decide whether to follow this path.

The implication of the *Gita* is that the path is one of several lives, or incarnations into physical existence. Through incarnation, if one is choosing to live this path, then one is purifying the soul until it is eventually at a level of godliness.

In ancient Egypt we find the idea of metempsychosis, where the soul may incarnate into other forms of life (such as animals) prior to another human incarnation.[159] Thus, the Greek philosophers—Empedocles, Plato, Socrates, Pythagoras etc., after studying ancient Egypt—came to a similar conclusion. Socrates explains that the soul is immortal and has been born many times, its destination to wisen until it becomes the hero and transcends birth.[160]

These Greek philosophers served as the basis of the foundation of modern science in the Western World. Scholars agree that Isaac Newton and Gottfried Wilhelm von Leibniz both discovered calculus independent of each other. Today, calculus is used in all areas of physics: space travel, astronomy, electromagnetism, general relativity, etc. And the founders of calculus both shared this understanding of reincarnation.

In his *New Essays Concerning Human Understanding,* Leibniz explains that the soul is immortal and that this spirit runs not only

---

[159] *Manners and Customs of the Ancient Egyptians, Volume 4* by Sir John Wilkinson, pg. 316 (Murray, 1847)
[160] *Essential Sacred Writing From Around the World* by Mircea Eliade, pgs. 377 (Harper & Row, 1992)

through humans, but plants, animals and all other life.[161] Leibniz understood that our souls reincarnate and writes about the details of what happens.

"If [souls] pass into a new body coarse or sensible, they would always preserve the expression of all that they had perceived in the old, and it would even be necessary for the new body to manifest it so that the individual continuity will always have its real marks. But whatever our past state may have been, the effect it leaves cannot always be for us *apperceivable*. [...] We see there by that the acts of an ancient might belong to a modern who had the same soul, although he did not perceive them. But if he should come to recognize it, still more would personal identity follow. For the rest *a portion of matter* passing from one body into another does not constitute the same human individual, nor what is called the *ego*, but it is the soul which constitutes it."[162]

In continuation, through Newton's alchemical studies he put Ovidian physics into practice.[163] Ovid's concept of physics was heavily influenced by a sorceress named Aia, who healed him of swollen legs, bleeding gums, and digestive problems after his exile. Ovid and Aia engage in what Theo Ziolkowsi terms a "Platonic *amor intellectualis*" and lived together many years. "During their time together she teaches Ovid about the religion of Zalmoxis, which amounts to an acceptance of death and the belief in reincarnation: the body is restored to the earth through burial

---

161 *New Essays Concerning Human Understanding* by Gottfried Wilhelm von Leibniz, pg. 68 (Open Court, 1949)
162 Ibid, pg. 251
163 *Supernatural Environments in Shakespeare's England* by Kristen Poole, pg. 50 (Cambridge University Press, 2011)

[...] and the spirit survives and returns in higher, purer forms."[164] Newton's alchemical initiations required delving into this concept, experimenting with nature to test the idea.

The idea is an archetypal pattern. Throughout the pre-colonized Americas we find reincarnation. As in other areas where we find reincarnation, there were certain souls (the shamans), who planned out their next lives—where they'll be born, which parents, etc., and through this cognition, evolution of the soul was consciously carried out.[165] A Winnebago shaman explained what happened before he was born:

> "I was brought down to earth. I did not enter a woman's womb, but I was taken into a room. There I remained, conscious at all times. One day I heard the noise of little children outside and some other sounds, so I thought I would go outside. Then it seemed to me that I went through a door, but I was really being born again from a woman's womb. As I walked out I was struck with the sudden rush of cold air and I began to cry."[166]

The transmigration of the soul and reincarnation shows up in other geographical locations. In the early 20th century, Professor Baldwin Spencer showed that the belief in reincarnation is found throughout the majority of tribes in Australia.[167] In Africa, we find this pattern as well; death allows the soul to reincarnate and

---

[164] *Ovid and the Moderns* by Theo Ziolkowsi, pg. 123 (Cornell University Press, 2005)
[165] Ibid, pgs. 187-93
[166] Ibid, pgs. 192-3
[167] *Native Tribes of the Northern Territory* of Australia by Baldwin Spencer, pg. 263 (Macmillan, 1914)

make amends to any past 'ills.'[168] In the Orient, reincarnation is found in every region (from North to South Asia). In the *Bön* tradition, the soul incarnates with its built up karmic energy, *la*, and aims to remove this karma and achieve Buddhahood.[169]

> "A form of reincarnation also occurred in Sámi tradition (of Scandinavia), by which a pregnant woman or shaman might see a vision of a dead relative in a dream and determine to name a new child after the deceased. This act was seen as allowing the dead to return to the family as a living member." (parenthesis are mine)[170]

The belief in reincarnation is also found in tribes throughout Africa.[171]

As this philosophical idea shows up on the six inhabitable continents, its idea deserves contemplation, followed by vigorous pursuit.

In the scheme of the heroic epic (regarding our present lives), this contemplation begets the realization of a sense of resurrection. In pursuing our inner heroic epic, death should not be restraining. Even if death comes before the ultimate victory, the actions one makes in this life toward achieving the final heroic goal will allow one to continue this progress in the next life. Thus,

---

[168] *The Oxford Encyclopedia of African Thought, Volume 1* eidted by Abiola Irele and Biodun Jeyifo, pgs. 351-2 (Oxford University Press, 2010)

[169] *Bθ & Bön* by Dmitry Ermakov, pg. 521 (Vajra Publications, 2010)

[170] *Nordic Religions in the Viking Age* by Thomas DuBois, pg. 75 (University of Pennsylvania Press, 1999)

[171] *Encyclopædia of Religion and Ethics: Suffering-Zwingli* by James Hastings, pg. 426 (T. & T. Clark, 1922)

the fear of death is an obstacle on the path—it must be relinquished.

PART THREE
Logos

7 YESTERDAY'S DRAGON

"The destruction of huge organizations will eventually prove to be a necessity because, like a cancerous growth, they eat away man's nature as soon as they become ends in themselves and attain autonomy. From that moment they grow beyond man and escape his control. He becomes their victim and is sacrificed to the madness of an idea that knows no master. All great organizations in which the individual no longer counts are exposed to this danger. There seems to be only one way of countering this threat to our lives, and that is the 'revaluation' of the individual." – Carl Jung[172]

To demonstrate the appearance of archetypes in history, we shall look over a specific time where they are rather apparent— the counterculture movement of the 60s and 70s. To do so, we first need to understand the setting leading up to this revolution so that the 'dragon' archetype is outlined. Then we shall identify the heroes, by showing *young* individuals who became pioneers of the movement and their methods for taking on the dragon. In

---

[172] *Flying Saucers* by C.G. Jung, pgs. 73-4 (Princeton University Press, 1978)

conclusion, we shall see that behind the scenes of these modern heroes were esoteric lives.

At the beginning of the twentieth century there were two dominant forces having a hegemony in the political economy of the United States of America: the J.P. Morgan group and the John D. Rockefeller group. John Rockefeller founded Standard Oil, which later split into Exxon, Chevron, Amoco, Mobil, and ConocoPhillips, among others; the Rockefeller group went into commercial banking, the military and arms industry, and also made alliances with the Kuhn, Loeb Company for investment banking, and with Harriman-Bush for railroads and steel.[173] The Morgan group were the top of the bankers, but also had interests in railroads, arms and manufacturing firms—at the turn of the century J.P. Morgan bought Andrew Carnegie's United States Steel Company, as well.

It is generally believed that these two groups clashed, that they were archrivals; however, these groups were quick to join together for implementing a centralized bank in the United States of America—demonstrating that tensions were not what they seem.[174] They formed a mutual board in order to execute this plan and by 1910,

> "[…] the financial power elite now had a bill. The significance of the composition of the small meeting must be stressed: two Rockefeller men (Aldrich and Vanderlip), two Morgans (Davison and Norton), one Kuhn, Loeb person (Warburg), and

---

[173] *A History of Money and Banking in the United States* by Murray Rothbard, pg. 188 (Ludwig von Mises Institute, 2002)
[174] Ibid.

one economist friendly to both camps (Andrew).[175]

In 1913, their bill, The Federal Reserve Act, was signed by Woodrow Wilson.[176] This act did many things: one, it created a 'permanent,' private and public centralized banking system in the U.S. that looked over all other banks; two, it created a single currency, the Federal Reserve Note; three, it allowed banks to establish branches in other countries; four, it made the printing of money for corporate concerns de facto—money that does not exist—"The primary purpose of the Federal Reserve Act of December 23, 1913, is to make certain that there will always be an available supply of money and credit in this country with which to meet unusual banking requirements."[177] Prior to the bill being passed, J.P. Morgan died in Rome, Italy, and the Rockefeller Foundation was founded. Despite J. P. Morgan's death, the alliance between the established Morgan group and the Rockefeller Group went on to define what is implied by "unusual banking requirements."

The next year, World War One broke out. Paul Warburg, who had previously worked for J.P. Morgan and Kuhn, Loeb and Company and was decorated by the German Kaiser, was appointed to be the Vice President of the Federal Reserve Board. Meanwhile, his brother Max Warburg was the "[...] head of the German banking firm Warburg and Company and financial adviser

---

[175] Ibid, pg. 253
[176] *A History of the Federal Reserve, Volume 2, Book 2* by Allan Meltzer, pg. 1218 (University of Chicago Press, 2010)
[177] *The Federal Reserve Act of 1913* by O. M. W. Sprague, pg. 213 in The Quarterly Journal of Economics, Vol. 28, No.2 (Oxford University Press, 1914)

to the German delegation."[178] Max Warburg met with the Kaiser of Germany to discuss finances throughout his time in Germany.[179] U.S. companies started trading with both the Central Powers and the Allied side. This continued until Britain's blockade in 1915, which stopped trade between the U.S. and Germany. The financial elite profited significantly during this time: "The New York Fed sold nearly half of all Treasury securities offered during the war; it handled most of the Treasury's foreign exchange business, and acted as a central depository of funds from other Federal Reserve banks."[180]

With both the Morgan group and the Rockefeller group having combined properties in copper, steel, railroads, banking institutions, oil, arms and other industrial trusts and trade ending between the U.S. and the Central Powers, bringing the United States into the war was their top priority. This would be the way to inaugurate an industrial military complex that would keep the "unusual banking requirements" rising exponentially. The highly decorated Major General, Smedley Butler, wrote:

"In the World War [One] a mere handful garnered the profits of the conflict. At least 21,000 new millionaires and billionaires were made in the United States during the World War. That many admitted their huge blood gains in their income tax returns. How many other war millionaires falsified

---

[178] *Social Discredit* by Janine Singel, pg. 42 (McGill-Queen's University Press, 2000)

[179] *The Origins of World War I* edited by Richard Hamilton and Holger Herwig, pg. 489 (Cambridge University Press, 2003)

[180] *A History of Money and Banking in the United States* by Murray Rothbard, pg. 371 (Ludwig von Mises Institute, 2002)

their tax returns no one knows."[181]

As a result, a new form of oligarchic classism was established—a tree diagram of corporations with the Morgan group and the Rockefeller group at the top. The war allowed for the federal government's power to become entirely corporatized. Federal agencies such as the Wars Industries Board, the Food Administration, the Fuel Administration, etc. were created, headed by corporate executives.[182]

After the war, America was reshaped into a new image. At first, the economy fell into a minor recession. Then American consumerism as we know it began, and industries boomed. In the 1920s, the fast rise of the Ku Klux Klan, a radical form of racism, was also brewing in America. The institutionalization of America as a reckoning global power sparked a Roman-like collective ego in the nation. Suddenly, the polar-opposite of the prosperous 20s manifested in the 30s. The wealth-level between the classes expanded for few, and vastly decreased for many, and then the Great Depression arrived.

In 1932, Congressman Louis T. McFadden brought formal charges against the Federal Reserve for several criminal acts. He addressed Congress with this statement:

"Some people think that the Federal Reserve Banks are United States Government institutions. They are private monopolies which prey upon the people of these United

---

[181] *War is a Racket: The Antiwar Classic by America's Most Decorated Soldier* by Smedley D. Butler, pg. 23 (Feral House, 2003)
[182] *Discontented America: The United States in the 1920s* by David Goldberg, pg. 10 (Johns Hopkins University Press, 1999)

States for the benefit of themselves and their foreign
customers; foreign and domestic speculators and swindlers;
and rich and predatory money lenders. In that dark crew of
financial pirates there are those who would cut a man's
throat to get a dollar out of his pocket; there are those who
send money into states to buy votes to control our
legislatures; there are those who maintain International
propaganda for the purpose of deceiving us into granting of
new concessions which will permit them to cover up their
past misdeeds and set again in motion their gigantic train of
crime."[183]

McFadden was the president of the First National Bank for nearly
a decade prior to making these charges, so his perspective on the
matter was held creditable. Other individuals, like Congressman
Carl Weideman and Representative William Lemke, aided
McFadden's attempt with their support. Lemke made this remark
in 1934 during a Congressional hearing:

"This nation is bankrupt; every State in this Union is bankrupt;
the people of the United States, as a whole, are bankrupt.
The public and private debts of this Nation, which are
evidenced by bonds, mortgages, notes, or other written
instruments amount to about $250,000,000,000, and it is
estimated that there is about $50,000,000,000 of which there
is no record, making in all about $300,000,000,000 of public
and private debts. The total physical cash value of all the
property in the United States is now estimated at about
$70,000,000,000. That is more than it would bring if sold at
public auction. In this we do not include debts or the
evidence of debts, such as bonds, mortgages, and so forth.

---

[183] Congressional Record, June 10th, 1932

These are not physical property. They will have to be paid out of the physical property. How are we going to pay $300,000,000,000 with only $70,000,000,000?"[184]

With some support, McFadden and his companions attacked the Federal Reserve, affirming that it had caused the Great Depression and funded the Bolshevik Revolution.
He stayed in office until 1935, and then a year later mysteriously died in a hotel in New York City. McFadden already had two assassinations attempts prior to this.[185] His death reeks of a successful third attempt.

During this decade, interesting events occurred in globalization's timeline. Both the Rockefeller group and J.P. Morgan and Company made business deals with what would become one of the dominant corporations of Nazi Germany, IG Farben.

"The axis of cooperation linking IG Farben and Standard Oil had as its primary business in the fuelling and provisioning of the war machine of the Third Reich. At Auschwitz, for instance, factories went up to the house complexes of potent new technology designed to transform coal into aviation fuel and the main ingredients of synthetic rubber."[186]

Simultaneously, Bush-Harriman became involved with two German companies: Vereinigte Stahlwerke AG, the largest steel

---

[184] Congressional Record, March, 3rd, 1934
[185] *Rise and fall of the United States, Volume 1* by National Voters Quorum, pg. 250 (National Voters Quorum, 1975)
[186] *Earth into Property: Colonization, Decolonization and Capitalism* by Anthony Hall, pg. 234 (McGill-Queen's University Press, 2010)

and coal company in Nazi Germany and the Consolidated Silesian Steel Company, which,

> "During the war, the company made use of Nazi slave labour from the concentration camps, including Auschwitz. The ownership of CSSC changed hands several times in the 1930s, but documents from the US National Archive declassified last year link Bush to CSSC."[187]

Other corporations, like Coca-Cola, Ford, GM, and IBM were involved with both sides. Coca-Cola used patriotic advertising propaganda to sell their products to both the Third-Reich and the Allied countries.[188]

WWII is what wholly actualized the Industrial Military Complex in America, while also bringing corporate consumerism to the next level. When the war was finally over, a new one was created—communism was the new scapegoat and the Soviet Union was the new enemy—this was the way to keep the unusual banking requirements, or neocolonialism, in full effect.

With the implementation of this scapegoat, right after the war, the U.S. government retrieved 1,600 scientists from Nazi Germany, under Operation Paperclip, to prevent access to their knowledge from the Soviet Union, the UK, and other countries.[189]

---

[187] *How Bush's grandfather helped Hitler's rise to power* by Ben Aris and Duncan Campbell from *The Guardian* (September 25th, 2004)
[188] *Coca-Cola Goes to War* by Eleanor Jones and Florian Ritzmann, at: http://xroads.virginia.edu/~CLASS/coke/coke2.html
[189] *Secret Agenda: The United States Government, Nazi Scientists, and Project Paperclip, 1944-1990* by Linda Hunt (St. Martin's University Press, 1991)

These scientists were then given new names, jobs, and lives in America, some of whom continued their controversial work under classified programs.

In 1947 the Central Intelligence Agency was created. Two years later, the CIA went into Syria and overthrew the democratically elected President, Shukri Quwatly, who was neutral to both capitalists and communists.[190] The CIA set up a regime led by the former Army Chief of Staff, Husni al-Za'im, who approved the Trans-Arabian Pipeline. This pipeline was built by a joint venture company that several Standard Oil companies collectively developed. This regime failed, however, and the covert operation continued for nearly a decade. Meanwhile, the democratically elected Prime Minster of Iran, Mohammad Mossadegh, was going to nationalize the oil industry. Under Operation Ajax, the CIA overthrew this government and replaced it with the former Shah regime, led by Mohammed Reza Pahlevi. With this *coup d'état* being successful, the Anglo-Iranian Oil Company that was extorting oil in the region changed its name to the British Petroleum Company. Similarly, the dictatorship that the American United Fruit Company set up in Guatemala failed and a democracy was birthed, which elected Jacobo Árbenz Guzmán as President. The United Fruit Company, which was controlled by the Rockefeller group[191], was losing the clench of its monopoly; so yet again, the CIA intervened.

"The Guatemala operation, known as PBSUCCESS, was both more ambitious and more thoroughly successful than either

---

[190] *1949-1958, Syria* by Professor Douglas Little in pgs. 12-3 of Press for Conversion (May 2003)
[191] *Launching Global Health* by Steven Palmer, pg. 63 (University of Michigan Press, 2010)

precedent (Syria or Iran). Rather than helping a prominent contender gain power with a few inducements, PBSUCCESS used an intensive paramilitary and psychological campaign to replace a popular, elected government with a political nonentity." (parenthesis are mine)[192]

While the CIA was securing neo-colonialism, the industrial military complex was growing. In 1950, the Chinese, Soviets, and North Koreans fought against the U.S., South Koreans, and the British—yet another war for power that also tested out the strength of the communist-threat scapegoat. This feud kept the industrial military complex on high production until the war's end in 1953.

Two years later, America's longest military conflict began to stir—the paradigm of seemingly, never-ending wars was enthralling the people. The production of Hydrogen bombs was gradually rising, and the communist scare was being implemented at such a level that its propaganda successfully controlled the psyches of the masses. One individual wrote, "My school had unsettling air raid drills, but I recall more vividly my terror of the citywide blackouts, when we had to cover our windows with blankets to ensure no enemy could find Fairbanks."[193] Besides a small population, the state of mind of most of the country was completely controlled by the status quo—despite the status quo being ridiculous, as a city covered in blankets would be more revealing to the enemy.

Many people's psychological states were quarantined by the

---

[192] *Secret History, Second Edition* by Nick Cullather, pg. 7 (Stanford University Press, 2006)
[193] *Psychological fallout,* by Michael Carey, pg. 20 in the *Bulletin of the Atomic Scientists* (Jan., 1982)

financial elite's propaganda. While a war was being fought against narcotics,"[...] advertisements in the 1950s hailed the arrival of "happy pills," "peace-of-mind drugs," and "miracle drugs." In 1957 physicians wrote more than 48 million prescriptions for tranquilizers; by 1967 more than two-thirds of prescriptions for psychoactive drugs were written for women."[194]

A new form of consumer capitalism propaganda was commenced in the mid-1950s, aimed to put America's economic system on a pedestal above all other countries.[195] Furthermore, nationalistic propaganda continued just as the wars did.

This is rather ironic because Nazi Germany also implemented these strategies. "At the height of the Nazi struggle against narcotic addiction, German pharmacology and the pharmaceutical industry were busy creating new generations of abusable drugs."[196] Nationalist propaganda in Nazi Germany was implemented in posters, films, newspapers, magazines, etc.[197] What was our government really doing with the 1,600 scientists from Nazi Germany?

The racism implemented in the United States demonstrates the features of the 'Roman' archetype that we saw in Chapter One that has also manifested in other locations: "One of the most

---

[194] *Drug Addiction Research & the Health of Women* edited by Cora Wetherington and Adele Roman, pg. 12 (Diane Publishing, 1999)

[195] *Measuring America* by Andrew Yarrow, pg. 134 (University of Massachusetts Press, 2010)

[196] *Germans on Drugs* by Robert Stephens, pg. 17 (University of Michigan Press, 2007)

[197] *Spaniards and Nazi Germany* by Wayne Bowen, pgs. 41-4 (University of Missouri Press, 2000)

influential British studies of race relations in the 1950s equated the Indian caste system with the 'so-called caste system in the Southern United States' and with the apartheid regime of South Africa."[198] An example of the U.S.'s imperial racism is demonstrated in the story of Emmett Till.

On August 27th, 1955, the young African-American, Emmett, recently arrived in Webb, Mississippi after taking the train from Chicago. He and some of his friends decided to skip Church and go to a grocery store. From here, Emmett purportedly flirted with a 24-year old white woman named Carolyn Bryant. The next day, her husband Roy Bryant and his half-brother J. W. Milam kidnapped Emmett from his great-uncle's house, took him to a barn near the Tallahassee River and beat him to mutilation; they gouged out one of his eyes, shot him through the head and then weighted him down by putting his head in a heavy fan-blade secured around his neck and head with barbed wire. The two men then threw Emmett in the river—his body being found days later.

On September 8th, 1955 the *Daily Worker* wrote:

"The mutilated body of 14-year-old Emmett Louis Till has been laid to rest in Chicago. But the racist conspiracy which set the stage for his murder, and those of two other Negroes, is still abroad in Mississippi and elsewhere. New Klan-like groups are still being formed. White-collared and well-tailored members of these groups are continuing to fan racial passions. And many state officials are using their position for

---

[198] *The Silent War* by Frank Füredi, pg. 228 (Rutgers University Press, 1998)

the same purpose."[199]

The jury for the murder trial dismissed Bryant and Milam of all charges, claiming lack of evidence.

This event was the last straw for many individuals; it was finally time to stand up against this state that people were living in.

With this brief summary of the decades leading up to the counterculture, we have identified the dragon.

Tolkien's dragon was a "Dark Lord" who destroys nature to build its power, kills for control, and seeks to control all of Middle-Earth. Imperialism, or the counterculture's dragon, has decimated the planet for resources to build its power, has killed countless people for power and control, and its process of globalization demonstrates neo-colonialism with an agenda to control the world.

The economic elite were also notorious for intermarriages between the families in power (Schiff, Warburg, Seligman, Loebs, Rockefeller, Stillman, etc.).[200]

"Marriages between wealthy Americans have, by all odds, been more significant. Any tendency toward dispersal of great wealth that might be expected from its supposed distribution among numerous offspring of unions between rich and poor has been more than offset by the actual

---

[199] *The Lynching of Emmett Till* edited by Christopher Metress, pg. 27 (University of Virginia Press, 2002)
[200] *A History of Money and Banking in the United States* by Murray Rothbard, pg. 207; 214-5; 234-5 (Ludwig von Mises Institute, 2002)

marriage of wealth with wealth. The wealthiest Americans, with few exceptions, are already joined by a multiplicity of family ties, just as they are joining by interlocking directorates and mutual participations in economic and social undertakings. The 'community of interest' of the rich to whom the elder J.P. Morgan made profound public obeisance has become, to a startling degree, a joint family interest."[201]

The imperialism of Rowling's dragon embodies this oligarchy, with the hierarchy of 'purebloods' with the Dark Lord at the top who spread their evil around the world.

---

[201] *America's 60 Families* by Ferdinand Lundberg, pg. 9 (Halcyon House, 1939)

8 THE HEROES

"One by one we get awakened by the sound of Krishna's flute. His flute works in many ways." George Harrison[202]

Amidst all of this chaos, a revolution was brewing amongst the youth. The 1950s brought along the Beatnik movement of anti-conformity. The product of this movement was open-minded individuals refusing the status quo and countering the culture.

What was needed next was a brigade of heroic leaders who could bestow this altered state of mind to the masses. A symbol with the power to encourage more souls to join the heroic adventure was needed.

There are many different figures from this time period who deserve notice for their efforts as an aspect of this symbol, but we shall focus only on a few of the iconic figures who will be familiar to the majority of readers to get the point across. All of these leaders of the counterculture movement were musicians, and we

---

[202] *Working Class Mystic* by Gary Tillery, pg. 1 (Quest Books, 2011)

shall see some interesting patterns that show up between their stories. In Part Two, we learned that sound and its vibrations are closely connected to the hero and performing magic. The *logos* of this statement will be demonstrated in this chapter.

Embodying the poetic demeanor of the Beatniks, Bob Dylan can be argued as a key, inducing figure in the counterculture—he certainly inspired all of the other 'heroes' that we will look into.

In interviews, the young Dylan insisted that he was not the leader of this anti-conformist movement. We will respect Dylan and not put him on the pedestal of sole leader. If Dylan was not the leader, however, he was a guide—an example. Dylan's being, alone, guided individuals into becoming their own leaders—to express their own individuality.

At an early age, Dylan decided that his life's passion was revolutionary at heart. Throughout Dylan's autobiography, he explains that he disagreed with and resented politics, wars, commercialism and the brute force of the imperialist Western hegemony, and he wanted to do something about it.[203] From this, he realized that national and corporate viewpoints were one big joke; they were fake. He wanted nothing to do with big-time record labels, for he thought that this 'elitist' music was watered down.[204] He writes, "I just thought of mainstream culture as lame as hell and a big trick."[205]

Dylan also started playing and writing music and writing poetry at a young age. Through epiphany, Dylan realized that

---

[203] *Chronicles, Volume 1* by Bob Dylan, pg. 4; 45 (Simon & Schuster, 2005)
[204] Ibid, pg. 5
[205] Ibid, pg. 45

through music and poetry he could make his stab at this 'dragon' of society. During the 60s, his music became popularized by several other popular artists.

Songs like: "The Times They Are a-Changin'," "Masters of War," "Talkin' World War III Blues," and "The Ballad of Emmett Till," reveals Dylan's counter to the culture. For example, in "Masters of War," Dylan sings:

> "Come you masters of war
>
> You that build all the guns
>
> You that build the death planes
>
> You that build all the bombs
>
> You that hide behind walls
>
> You that hide behind desks
>
> I just want you to know
>
> I can see through your masks."

Dylan also helped bring the story of Emmitt Till to publicity (even though it is 'forgotten' by many history books of today). His song emotionally grasps the listener, while explaining the atrocities that happened to Till. Its overall message is: 'if you've been touched by this story then do something about already!' The intentions of Dylan's early music were clearly against the imperialistic archetype.

What is interesting about Dylan's story is that we see the same mythological elements unfold in his life that we see in the mythologies from around the world and the mythologies of

Rowling and Tolkien.

Dylan experienced an expansion of his consciousness in his early years.[206] "It wasn't money or love that I was looking for. I had a heightened sense of awareness, was set in my ways, impractical and a visionary to boot."[207] Through this expansion of consciousness, Dylan studied esoteric and occult ideas. In the rhetoric of his autobiography, he references alchemy,[208] shamanism,[209] reincarnation,[210] and causing magic through sound vibrations.

"I felt right at home in this mythical realm made up not with individuals so much as archetypes, vividly drawn archetypes of humanity, metaphysical in shape, each rugged soul filled with natural knowing and inner wisdom."[211]

We also find the element of supernatural guidance within Dylan's story. Dylan explains that he felt as if he had angels communicating with his psyche.[212] He also explains that music sent him into hypnotic, trance states.[213] We can see the similarities between Dylan and the shamans from around the world. Dylan writes,

"You've got to have power and dominion over the spirits. I had done it once, and once was enough. Someone would come along eventually who would have it again—someone

---

[206] Ibid, pg. 77
[207] Ibid, pg. 9
[208] Ibid, pg. 37; 121
[209] Ibid, pg. 13; 186
[210] Ibid, pg. 180; 242
[211] Ibid, pg. 236
[212] Ibid, pg.146
[213] Ibid, pg. 161

who could see into things, the truth of things—not metaphorically, either—but really see, like seeing into metal and making it melt, see it for what it was and reveal it for what it was, with hard words and vicious insight."[214]

Behind Dylan's popularity was a wizard casting spells in the form of musical poetry.

Dylan's importance in the counterculture cannot be denied, as his work influenced the next figure.[215] With more people combating the racism of the apartheid-like segregation in America, what was needed was a part Native-American, part African-American, to completely transcend barriers and express individuality.

The young James Marshall 'Jimi' Hendrix had very similar views as Dylan on the imperialism archetype. He explained that most of the people in America are like sheep.[216] "The world's nothin' but a big gimmick—wars, napalm bombs and all that, people get burned up on TV and it's nothin' but a big gimmick."[217] Hendrix explained that we need to have harmony between humans and the earth, and we're destroying this harmony by dumping garbage in the ocean and polluting the air; we need to remove the evil that the thirst for money will always create.[218]

"I think America has on its mind to let other groups really suffer badly and then put them away somewhere. It's very

---

[214] Ibid, pg. 219
[215] *Hendrix on Hendrix: Interviews and Encounters with Jimi Hendrix* edited by Steven Roby, pg. 229 (Chicago Review Press, 2012)
[216] Ibid, pg. 134
[217] Ibid, pg. 326
[218] Ibid, pg. 149; 195

sick, but that's what I think is going on. Some people around here are naturally sick in the head anyway. And half of those people are running [the country]."[219]

This understanding led Hendrix to resent the establishment and to promote an alternative in his music. "We plan for our sound to go inside the soul of the person, actually, and see if they can awaken some kind of thing in their minds 'cause there's so many sleeping people."[220]

When the media attempted to label Hendrix as 'moody' he suavely responded,

"The establishment [projects] a certain image and if it works, they have it made. They knock down somebody else for instance, you know, like saying I'm moody or so-and-so is evil or saying blah blah, woof woof is a maniac or something, so that everybody gets scared to actually know about me. So that's part of the establishment's games."[221]

Hendrix's image, expressing its individuality (i.e. wearing clothes that fulfilled his dreams, despite what other people thought of them)—along with his powerful sound—allowed him to gain popularity and influence the masses.

Like Dylan, Hendrix also had a very metaphysical life. Hendrix believed that everyone is a temple of God.

"I am electric religion—because it is all about religion, not Christianity. It was the Christians who started most of the wars in this world. I see in front of me a universal religion,

---

[219] Ibid, pg. 149
[220] Ibid, pg. 203
[221] Ibid, pg. 168

containing all beliefs, containing the essence of them all. In that religion the children can grow up and feel free, they will not be programmed, like they are today."[222]

Then there is the metaphysical guidance. Hendrix once had a dream that he was at a pyramid in ancient Egypt, and thought that he was visiting a past-life of his. In fact, in interviews, Hendrix noted his belief that death is the end and the beginning. He also constantly had visions that guided him to the 'something bigger'.[223]

These visions allowed Hendrix to embody the heroic archetype to change society. He understood that revolutions throughout history usually occur when art and/or music trigger a movement. He foresaw music to be the catalyst for the next big, global change,[224] for Hendrix believed that sound waves are a cosmic, powerful phenomenon.

"Music is magic. Already this idea of living today is magic. There's a lot of sacrifices to make. I'm workin' on music to be completely, utterly a magic science, where it's all pure positive. It can't work if it's not positive."[225]

While the Americans Bob Dylan and Jimi Hendrix were breaking down standards in America, the young British heroes were rising to influence as well.

The lives of John Lennon and George Harrison of the Beatles reveal rebellious childhoods. Both individuals were constantly in

---

[222] Ibid pg. 298
[223] Ibid, pg. 195
[224] Ibid, pg. 286
[225] *The Superstars in their own words* by Douglas Hall and Sue Clark, pg. 23 (Music Sales, 1970)

detention for their status-quo-refusing manners. This outlook at a young age enabled them to refuse to conform to the status quo once they achieved popularity. Lennon writes,

> "The people who are in control and in power and the class system and the whole bullshit bourgeois scene is exactly the same. We've grown up a little, all of us, and there has been a change and we are a bit freer and all that, but it's the same game. Nothing's really changed. It's the same! They're doing exactly the same things, selling arms to South Africa, killing blacks in the streets. It just makes you puke, and I woke up to that."[226]

Lennon was the biggest activist out of the group.

In 1970, Lennon protested with thousands of people against the British government's trial against a counterculture magazine; he carried a sign saying "For the IRA, Against British Imperialism." In 1971 Lennon protested the government's takeover of the Onondaga First Peoples' land, with a group of Onondaga Native Americans. Lennon sent back his 'Member of the Most Excellent Order of the British Empire' award, that Queen of England gave to him, with a note protesting imperialism, such as the involvement in Vietnam.

> "He publicly supported the takeover of shipyards in Scotland by eight thousand laid-off workers. Rather than submit to a cost-saving measure, they refused to give up their jobs and moved in to occupy the factories. Lennon contributed a thousand pounds one week to their relief fund."

---

[226] *Lennon Remembers* edited by Jann Wenner, pgs. 106-7 (Verso, 2001)

Lennon was also very active in fighting against racism. For example, he tried to counter what the politician, Enoch Powell, was propagating about different races to the people and he supported the 'Harlem Six.' The other members of the Beatles were not as politically active, but still supported many of Lennon's viewpoints and gave a lot to Civil Rights charities.

The metaphysics of the Beatles did not sprout until Lennon and Harrison unwillingly took LSD. This was a transcendental experience for each, who turned on the other members to LSD afterwards. The following quotes show the similar effects LSD had on them. Lennon said, "God isn't in a pill, but LSD explained the mystery of life. It was a religious experience."[227] Paul McCartney said, "God is in everything. God is in the space between us. God is in the table in front of you. For me it just happens that I realized all this through acid."[228] And Harrison said,

> "I could see the sap running through the trees and everything and I just knew there was such a thing as God. I suddenly felt happy that we were all connected to that energy. . . . The energy within me and the energy within you is all the same. . . and I could see the space between us was buzzing too!"[229]

These mystical experiences of theirs changed the way they expressed who they were to the outer-world. The Beatles began dwelling into the occult and esotericism—from *The Tibetan Book of the Dead*, *The Bhagavad Gita*, and the *I Ching*, to *Raja* and *Kriya* Yoga, to Aleister Crowley, Carl Jung, and Wilhelm Reich. They

---

[227] *The Gospel According to the Beatles* by Steve Turner, pg. 111 (Westminster John Knox, 2006)
[228] Ibid.
[229] *George Harrison: His Words, Wit & Wisdom*, pg. 46 (Belmo Publishing, 2002)

were searching for more information on what they had experienced.

Lennon and Harrison began to realize that there was a destiny to their story and lives. They were bridging into the supernatural. "Lennon was fascinated with what he labeled magic—that is, the utilization of the omnipresent 'power' that he equated with God and that he thought would one day be understood scientifically."[230] Harrison explained it in a different way,

> "The energy is latent within everybody. It's there anyway. . . . Meditation is a natural process of being able to contact that, so by doing it each day you contact that energy and give yourself a little more. Consequently, you're able to do whatever you normally do—just with a little more happiness."[231]

This idea that God is something that was within themselves allowed them to broaden their expression for the need for individuality.

> "Produce your own dream. If you want to save Peru, go save Peru. It's quite possible to do anything, but not if you put it on the leader. Don't expect Carter or Reagan or John Lennon or Yoko Ono or Bob Dylan or Jesus Christ to come and do it for you. You have to do it yourself. That's what the great masters and mistresses have been saying ever since time began. They can point the way, leave signposts and little

---

[230] *The Cynical Idealist* by Gary Tillery, pg. 127 (Quest Books, 2009)
[231] *Working Class Mystic* by Gary Tillery, pg. 62 (Quest Books, 2011)

instructions in various books that are now called holy and worshiped for the cover of the book and not what it says, but the instructions are all there for all to see, have always been and always will be. There's nothing new under the sun. All the roads lead to Rome. And people cannot provide it for you. I can't wake you up. *You* can wake you up. I can can't cure you. *You* can cure you."[232]

Meanwhile, another group of British youth were embodying this mystical paragon into their music even further.

Led Zeppelin, lead by the young Jimmy Page, was completely rooted in esotericism. In an interview in 1974, Jimmy Page explains that he has been drawn to the occult ever since he was a little kid, and in particular, he was drawn to Magick. He explains that he's not into Satanism at all, but the idea that the magical experience—causing change through consciousness at will—is a living, indubitable phenomenon. Jimmy Page owned an occult bookshop filled with some of the most rare esoteric books at the time. He ended up buying and living in the old estate of the neo-Rosicrucian and much confused Aleister Crowley. Page explains,

'I feel Aleister Crowley is a misunderstood genius of the 20th century. Because his whole thing was liberation of the person, of the entity and that restrictions would foul you up, lead to frustration which leads to violence, crime, mental breakdown, depending on what sort of makeup you have underneath. The further this age we're in now gets into technology and alienation, a lot of the points he's made seem to manifest themselves all down the line.... I'm not saying it's

[232] *John Lennon and Yoko Ono* by David Sheff, pgs. 143-4 (Berkley Books, 1983)

a system for anybody to follow. I don't agree with everything but I find a lot of it relevant and it's those things that people attacked him on, so he was misunderstood.... I'm not trying to interest anyone in Aleister Crowley any more than I am in Charles Dickens. All it was, was that at a particular time he was expounding a theory of self-liberation, which is something which is so important. He was like an eye to the world, into the forthcoming situation. My studies have been quite intensive, but I don't particularly want to go into it because it's a personal thing and isn't in relation to anything apart from the fact that I've employed his system in my own day to day life....The thing is to come to terms with one's free will, discover one's place and what one is, and from that you can go ahead and do it and not spend your whole life suppressed and frustrated. It's very basically coming to terms with yourself."[233]

Page saw Led Zeppelin to be composed of 'four elements' (the members of the band), where the hidden, fifth element, manifested itself in Magick. The sounds of the band as a whole is what transmigrated this Magick onto others. Page remains convinced that the occult talismanic features that he Magickally willed into being, was what helped them rise to lionization. Thus, Page and the other members created alchemical hieroglyphs to express this symbol.

We find the same philosophy in Page that we find in the other young heroes of the counterculture. In 2008, Page explained,

"Enlightenment can be achieved at any point in time; it

---

[233] From the magazine *Sounds* (March 13, 1978)

just depends on when you want to access it. In other words you can always see truth; but do you recognize it when you see it or do you have to reflect back on it later?"[234]

Jimmy Page and Robert Plant also explained how the lyrics to their songs would just flow through them, as if they were 'channeling something higher'; yet they had already experienced this something higher. We see what is meant by 'higher' in the song "Kashmir":

"I am a traveler of both time and space, to be where I have been

To sit with elders of the gentle race, this world has seldom seen

They talk of days for which they sit and wait and all will be revealed. . . ."

"Stairway to Heaven" is one of the songs that Plant 'channeled.' This song is, of course, a prophecy of the period of 'utopia' that they saw to come after the 'dragon' is slayed.

"And it's whispered that soon, if we all call the tune,

Then the piper will lead us to reason.

And a new day will dawn for those who stand long,

And the forests will echo with laughter.

If there's a bustle in your hedgerow, don't be alarmed now,

---

[234] *Guitar World* (January, 2008)

It's just a spring clean for the May queen.

Yes, there are two paths you can go by, but in the long run

There's still time to change the road you're on.

And it makes me wonder.

Your head is humming and it won't go, in case you don't know,

The piper's calling you to join him,

Dear lady, can you hear the wind blow, and did you know

Your stairway lies on the whispering wind?

And as we wind on down the road

Our shadows taller than our soul.

There walks a lady we all know

Who shines white light and wants to show

How everything still turns to gold.

And if you listen very hard

The tune will come to you at last.

When all are one and one is all

To be a rock and not to roll."

9 CONJUNCTIO

*"Don't adventures ever have an end? I suppose not.
Someone else always has to carry on the story."*
- J.R.R. Tolkien[235]

We have seen that each of these individuals not only saw the imperialist archetype present in the countries that they lived in, but that they aimed to counter it. We have also seen that these individuals experienced an inflation of consciousness, and that there were cases of 'supernatural guidance' for each. We have seen all of the elements of the heroic myth incarnate in recent history.

Of course, there were many other young heroes besides these musicians who played their role in the greater counterculture movement. And the stories of, for example, Neil Young, Bob Marley, the members of RUSH and Pink Floyd, etc., would show the same mystical *gnosis* and revolutionary spirit. There are also many other members not falling into the youthful

---

[235] *The Lord of the Rings: The Fellowship of the Ring* by J.R.R. Tolkien, pg. 280 (Ballantine Books)

category who played their role in the counterculture—individuals such as Philip Berrigan, Betty Friedan, Olympia Brown, Rosa Parks, Carl Oglesby, Martin Luther King Jr., César Chávez and Harvey Milk. However, we do not need to analyze their lives, as we have already accomplished the objective with the individuals already outlined.

These young heroes broke down barriers; more importantly, they made it 'cool' to counter the culture—cool to express individuality.

Many youth of today take for granted so-called freedoms, privileges, and lifestyles that were products of this counterculture movement. No longer is it the social norm to dress utterly conservatively or to have the same hairstyle as everyone else. No longer are non-Caucasians looked upon as lesser-human beings and segregated from society at the same level that they were. No longer are women household objects. No longer is the expression of sexuality shunned. The times they have a-changed.

But have they truly changed? The same imperialist archetype is still evident in our society. Some scholars argue that the counterculture was a complete failure. I would not go as far as saying that. On the contrary, the counterculture accomplished exactly what it needed to. It kept the heroic myth alive for the time when the children of the sun shall awaken once more, blowing in as a storm that will shake the very foundation of the establishment, bringing it crashing down. This counterculture was a trial and error, in which, we now have proof in the power of the youth.

It is thus the responsibility of the student of *Esoteric Science* to embody the heroic archetype and make his or her own stab at the dragon. This doesn't mean a violent approach or that one has to do what Bob Dylan or John Lennon did. The answer is, indeed, much more simple: what can one do—while exhausting all of one's energy towards it—to make this world a better place? To sow a land where our children's children will be able to live? What can one do to carry on the adventures of these heroes?

AFTERWORD

Myths are unfathomable until they have been experienced. At the same time, one must question the myth. Is it real? The answer requires action. If one does not attempt to live the myth by concentrating his or her best efforts on the matter, then the answer will never be known. The next volume of this series is going to provide potential methods for this discernment—the initiations of the esoteric traditions and the techniques for expanding consciousness.

Volume 3 will look into my personal story, along with interviews from other young individuals whom I have known most of my life or whom I have met recently, and how there are patterns that show up between our experiences. It will show that there *is* a psychological phenomenon occurring amongst many of our youth today, that appears to be leading to something bigger.

This volume will also look into information adhering to the psychedelic experience. We saw how LSD completely changed the thought modalities and practices of the members of the Beatles (and this happened to many other monumental artists, such as Hendrix). In the next volume, we will see sound evidence as to why these experiences moved their lives so much. We will see that psychedelics have a lush history behind the religious experience—from Medieval Europe to Medieval India to the indigenous cultures on every continent.

Then we will look into methods for expanding, altering, and traveling within one's consciousness. In theory, this following volume will bring all of the information from these first two volumes into a practical perspective—what one can do to make the esoteric, exoteric.

30106162R00087

Made in the USA
Charleston, SC
04 June 2014